Connected  Mathematics™

Filling and Wrapping

Three-Dimensional Measurement

Teacher's Edition

Glenda Lappan
James T. Fey
William M. Fitzgerald
Susan N. Friel
Elizabeth Difanis Phillips

Developed at Michigan State University

DALE SEYMOUR PUBLICATIONS®
MENLO PARK, CALIFORNIA

Connected Mathematics™ was developed at Michigan State University with financial support from the Michigan State University Office of the Provost, Computing and Technology, and the College of Natural Science.

This material is based upon work supported by the National Science Foundation under Grant No. MDR 9150217.

This project was supported, in part,
by the
National Science Foundation
Opinions expressed are those of the authors
and not necessarily those of the Foundation

The Michigan State University authors and administration have agreed that all MSU royalties arising from this publication will be devoted to purposes supported by the Department of Mathematics and the MSU Mathematics Education Enrichment Fund.

This book is published by Dale Seymour Publications,® an imprint of Addison Wesley Longman, Inc.

Dale Seymour Publications
125 Greenbush Road South
Orangeburg, NY 10962
Customer Service: 800 872-1100

Managing Editor: Catherine Anderson
Project Editor: Stacey Miceli
Book Editor: Mali Apple
ESL Consultant: Nancy Sokol Green
Production/Manufacturing Director: Janet Yearian
Production/Manufacturing Coordinators: Claire Flaherty, Alan Noyes
Design Manager: John F. Kelly
Photo Editor: Roberta Spieckerman
Design: Don Taka
Composition: London Road Design, Palo Alto, CA
Electronic Prepress Revision: A. W. Kingston Publishing Services, Chandler, AZ
Illustrations: Pauline Phung, Margaret Copeland, Ray Godfrey
Cover: Ray Godfrey

Photo Acknowledgements: 5 © Kathy McLaughlin/The Image Works; 16 © David Shopper/Stock, Boston; 20 © Phyllis Graber Jensen/Stock, Boston; 21 Courtesy of the Pontiac Stadium Building Authority; 37 © Gary Benson/Tony Stone Images; 43 © Steve Kaufman/Peter Arnold, Inc.; 47 © Jean-Claude Lejeune/Stock, Boston; 53 (igloo) © Dave Rosenberg/Tony Stone Images; 53 (adobe) © Superstock, Inc.; 55 © Topham/The Image Works; 71 © Lionel Delevingne/Stock, Boston

DALE
SEYMOUR
PUBLICATIONS®

This Book is Printed
on Recycled Paper

Order number 45835
ISBN 1-57232-640-9

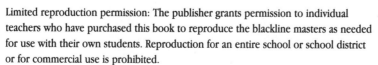
2 3 4 5 6 7 8 9 10-ML-01 00 99 98

The Connected Mathematics Project Staff

Project Directors

James T. Fey
University of Maryland

William M. Fitzgerald
Michigan State University

Susan N. Friel
University of North Carolina at Chapel Hill

Glenda Lappan
Michigan State University

Elizabeth Difanis Phillips
Michigan State University

Project Manager

Kathy Burgis
Michigan State University

Technical Coordinator

Judith Martus Miller
Michigan State University

Collaborating Teachers/Writers

Mary K. Bouck
Portland, Michigan

Jacqueline Stewart
Okemos, Michigan

Curriculum Development Consultants

David Ben-Chaim
Weizmann Institute

Alex Friedlander
Weizmann Institute

Eleanor Geiger
University of Maryland

Jane Mitchell
University of North Carolina at Chapel Hill

Anthony D. Rickard
Alma College

Evaluation Team

Mark Hoover
Michigan State University

Diane V. Lambdin
Indiana University

Sandra K. Wilcox
Michigan State University

Judith S. Zawojewski
National-Louis University

Graduate Assistants

Scott J. Baldridge
Michigan State University

Angie S. Eshelman
Michigan State University

M. Faaiz Gierdien
Michigan State University

Jane M. Keiser
Indiana University

Angela S. Krebs
Michigan State University

James M. Larson
Michigan State University

Ronald Preston
Indiana University

Tat Ming Sze
Michigan State University

Sarah Theule-Lubienski
Michigan State University

Jeffrey J. Wanko
Michigan State University

Field Test Production Team

Katherine Oesterle
Michigan State University

Stacey L. Otto
University of North Carolina at Chapel Hill

Teacher/Assessment Team

Kathy Booth
Waverly, Michigan

Anita Clark
Marshall, Michigan

Julie Faulkner
Traverse City, Michigan

Theodore Gardella
Bloomfield Hills, Michigan

Yvonne Grant
Portland, Michigan

Linda R. Lobue
Vista, California

Suzanne McGrath
Chula Vista, California

Nancy McIntyre
Troy, Michigan

Mary Beth Schmitt
Traverse City, Michigan

Linda Walker
Tallahassee, Florida

Software Developer

Richard Burgis
East Lansing, Michigan

Development Center Directors

Nicholas Branca
San Diego State University

Dianne Briars
Pittsburgh Public Schools

Frances R. Curcio
New York University

Perry Lanier
Michigan State University

J. Michael Shaughnessy
Portland State University

Charles Vonder Embse
Central Michigan University

Field Test Coordinators

Michelle Bohan
Queens, New York

Melanie Branca
San Diego, California

Alecia Devantier
Shepherd, Michigan

Jenny Jorgensen
Flint, Michigan

Sandra Kralovec
Portland, Oregon

Sonia Marsalis
Flint, Michigan

William Schaeffer
Pittsburgh, Pennsylvania

Karma Vince
Toledo, Ohio

Virginia Wolf
Pittsburgh, Pennsylvania

Shirel Yaloz
Queens, New York

Student Assistants

Laura Hammond
David Roche
Courtney Stoner
Jovan Trpovski
Julie Valicenti
Michigan State University

Patricia Wagner
Holmes Middle School

Greg Williams
Gundry Elementary School

Lansing

Susan Bissonette
Waverly Middle School

Kathy Booth
Waverly East Intermediate School

Carole Campbell
Waverly East Intermediate School

Gary Gillespie
Waverly East Intermediate School

Denise Kehren
Waverly Middle School

Virginia Larson
Waverly East Intermediate School

Kelly Martin
Waverly Middle School

Laurie Metevier
Waverly East Intermediate School

Craig Paksi
Waverly East Intermediate School

Tony Pecoraro
Waverly Middle School

Helene Rewa
Waverly East Intermediate School

Arnold Stiefel
Waverly Middle School

Portland

Bill Carlton
Portland Middle School

Kathy Dole
Portland Middle School

Debby Flate
Portland Middle School

Yvonne Grant
Portland Middle School

Terry Keusch
Portland Middle School

John Manzini
Portland Middle School

Mary Parker
Portland Middle School

Scott Sandborn
Portland Middle School

Shepherd

Steve Brant
Shepherd Middle School

Marty Brock
Shepherd Middle School

Cathy Church
Shepherd Middle School

Ginny Crandall
Shepherd Middle School

Craig Ericksen
Shepherd Middle School

Natalie Hackney
Shepherd Middle School

Bill Hamilton
Shepherd Middle School

Julie Salisbury
Shepherd Middle School

Sturgis

Sandra Allen
Eastwood Elementary School

Margaret Baker
Eastwood Elementary School

Steven Baker
Eastwood Elementary School

Keith Barnes
Sturgis Middle School

Wilodean Beckwith
Eastwood Elementary School

Darcy Bird
Eastwood Elementary School

Bill Dickey
Sturgis Middle School

Ellen Eisele
Sturgis Middle School

James Hoelscher
Sturgis Middle School

Richard Nolan
Sturgis Middle School

J. Hunter Raiford
Sturgis Middle School

Cindy Sprowl
Eastwood Elementary School

Leslie Stewart
Eastwood Elementary School

Connie Sutton
Eastwood Elementary School

Traverse City

Maureen Bauer
Interlochen Elementary School

Ivanka Berskshire
East Junior High School

Sarah Boehm
Courtade Elementary School

Marilyn Conklin
Interlochen Elementary School

Nancy Crandall
Blair Elementary School

Fran Cullen
Courtade Elementary School

Eric Dreier
Old Mission Elementary School

Lisa Dzierwa
Cherry Knoll Elementary School

Ray Fouch
West Junior High School

Ed Hargis
Willow Hill Elementary School

Richard Henry
West Junior High School

Dessie Hughes
Cherry Knoll Elementary School

Ruthanne Kladder
Oak Park Elementary School

Bonnie Knapp
West Junior High School

Sue Laisure
Sabin Elementary School

Stan Malaski
Oak Park Elementary School

Jody Meyers
Sabin Elementary School

Marsha Myles
East Junior High School

Mary Beth O'Neil
Traverse Heights Elementary School

Jan Palkowski
East Junior High School

Karen Richardson
Old Mission Elementary School

Kristin Sak
Bertha Vos Elementary School

Mary Beth Schmitt
East Junior High School

Mike Schrotenboer
Norris Elementary School

Gail Smith
Willow Hill Elementary School

Karrie Tufts
Eastern Elementary School

Mike Wilson
East Junior High School

Tom Wilson
West Junior High School

Minnesota

Minneapolis

Betsy Ford
Northeast Middle School

New York

East Elmhurst

Allison Clark
Louis Armstrong Middle School

Dorothy Hershey
Louis Armstrong Middle School

J. Lewis McNeece
Louis Armstrong Middle School

Rossana Perez
Louis Armstrong Middle School

Merna Porter
Louis Armstrong Middle School

Marie Turini
Louis Armstrong Middle School

North Carolina

Durham

Everly Broadway
Durham Public Schools

Thomas Carson
Duke School for Children

Mary Hebrank
Duke School for Children

Bill O'Connor
Duke School for Children

Ruth Pershing
Duke School for Children

Peter Reichert
Duke School for Children

Elizabeth City

Rita Banks
Elizabeth City Middle School

Beth Chaundry
Elizabeth City Middle School

Amy Cuthbertson
Elizabeth City Middle School

Deni Dennison
Elizabeth City Middle School

Jean Gray
Elizabeth City Middle School

John McMenamin
Elizabeth City Middle School

Nicollette Nixon
Elizabeth City Middle School

Malinda Norfleet
Elizabeth City Middle School

Joyce O'Neal
Elizabeth City Middle School

Clevie Sawyer
Elizabeth City Middle School

Juanita Shannon
Elizabeth City Middle School

Terry Thorne
Elizabeth City Middle School

Rebecca Wardour
Elizabeth City Middle School

Leora Winslow
Elizabeth City Middle School

Franklinton

Susan Haywood
Franklinton Elementary School

Clyde Melton
Franklinton Elementary School

Louisburg

Lisa Anderson
Terrell Lane Middle School

Jackie Frazier
Terrell Lane Middle School

Pam Harris
Terrell Lane Middle School

Ohio

Toledo

Bonnie Bias
Hawkins Elementary School

Marsha Jackish
Hawkins Elementary School

Lee Jagodzinski
DeVeaux Junior High School

Norma J. King
Old Orchard Elementary School

Margaret McCready
Old Orchard Elementary School

Carmella Morton
DeVeaux Junior High School

Karen C. Rohrs
Hawkins Elementary School

Marie Sahloff
DeVeaux Junior High School

L. Michael Vince
McTigue Junior High School

Brenda D. Watkins
Old Orchard Elementary School

Oregon

Canby

Sandra Kralovec
Ackerman Middle School

Portland

Roberta Cohen
Catlin Gabel School

David Ellenberg
Catlin Gabel School

Sara Normington
Catlin Gabel School

Karen Scholte-Arce
Catlin Gabel School

West Linn

Marge Burack
Wood Middle School

Tracy Wygant
Athey Creek Middle School

Pennsylvania

Pittsburgh

Sheryl Adams
Reizenstein Middle School

Sue Barie
Frick International Studies Academy

Suzie Berry
Frick International Studies Academy

Richard Delgrosso
Frick International Studies Academy

Janet Falkowski
Frick International Studies Academy

Joanne George
Reizenstein Middle School

Harriet Hopper
Reizenstein Middle School

Chuck Jessen
Reizenstein Middle School

Ken Labuskes
Reizenstein Middle School

Barbara Lewis
Reizenstein Middle School

Sharon Mihalich
Reizenstein Middle School

Marianne O'Connor
Frick International Studies Academy

Mark Sammartino
Reizenstein Middle School

Washington

Seattle

Chris Johnson
University Preparatory Academy

Rick Purn
University Preparatory Academy

Contents

In the grade 6 unit *Covering and Surrounding*, students developed strategies for measuring the perimeter and area of polygons and irregular figures. In *Filling and Wrapping*, students continue their study of measurement, using their understanding of perimeter and area in two dimensions to help them explore and develop the concepts of surface area and volume in three dimensions.

In this unit, students are introduced to volume as a measure of *filling* and to surface area as a measure of *wrapping*. After developing strategies for measuring the surface areas and volumes of rectangular prisms, students use their new knowledge to develop strategies for measuring the surface areas and volumes of cylinders, cones, spheres, and irregular solids. They also study the relationships between surface area and volume.

Packaging, the environment, and consumer purchases are some of the situations that students explore in this unit, through the consideration of questions such as the following:

- Baseballs, basketballs, and soccer balls are often packaged in boxes shaped liked cubes. What are the possible dimensions of a shipping box that would hold a given number of basketballs (in their boxes)? Which box would require the least amount of material?
- When you buy soft drinks or popcorn at a movie theater, you often have a choice of several sizes. How do the differences in price of the various sizes relate to the amount of soft drink or popcorn in the container?
- A spherical scoop of frozen yogurt is sitting in a cone. If the yogurt melts, will it fill the cone?
- We often throw away the packaging material from things we consume, such as shoes and cereal and light bulbs. Waste is filling our landfills at an alarming rate. How much waste do you think is produced by a typical American each year?
- What is the least amount of material required to construct a box with a specific volume? What characteristics would this box have?
- If a certain compost box will decompose a half pound of garbage per day, what size box is needed to decompose a pound of garbage each day?

In *Filling and Wrapping,* students explore the surface areas and volumes of rectangular prisms and cylinders in depth. They look informally at how changing the scale of a box affects its surface area and volume. They also informally investigate other solids—including cones, spheres, and irregular shapes—to develop volume relationships.

Rectangular Prisms

Students begin by exploring the surface area of a rectangular box. The strategy for finding the surface area of a box is to determine the total area needed to *wrap* the container. Students create flat patterns that can be folded into boxes. The area of the flat pattern becomes the surface area of the box. This provides a visual representation of surface area as a two-dimensional attribute, though it is an attribute of a three-dimensional object.

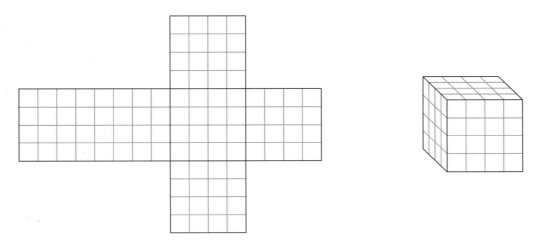

The strategy for finding the volume of a rectangular box is to count the number of layers of unit cubes it takes to *fill* the container. The number of unit cubes in a layer is equal to the area of the base—one unit cube sits on each square unit in the base. The volume of a rectangular prism is the area of its base multiplied by its height.

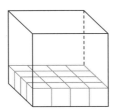

The same layering strategy is used to generalize the method for finding the volume of any prism. The volume of any prism is the area of its base multiplied by its height.

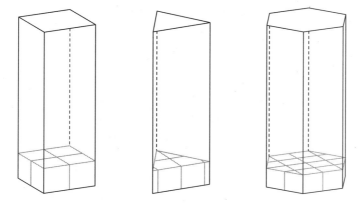

Cylinders

The surface area and volume of a cylinder are developed in a similar way. Students cut and fold a flat pattern to form a cylinder. In the process, they discover that the surface area of the cylinder is the area of the rectangle that forms the lateral surface plus the areas of the two circular ends.

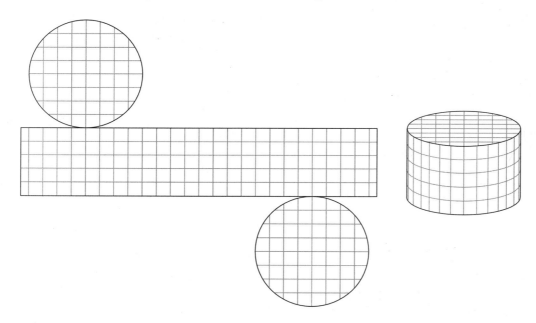

The volume of a cylinder is developed as the number of unit cubes in one layer (the area of the circular base) multiplied by the number of layers (the height) needed to fill the cylinder. Because the edges of the circular base cut through the unit cubes, students will have to estimate the number of cubes in the bottom layer.

Estimate the number
of units cubes in one layer,

and multiply by
the number of layers.

Cones and Spheres

Students conduct an experiment to demonstrate the relationships among the volumes of a cylinder, a cone, and a sphere. If all three have the same radius and the same height (the height being equal to two radii), then it takes three cones full of sand to fill the cylinder, and one and a half spheres full of sand to fill the cylinder.

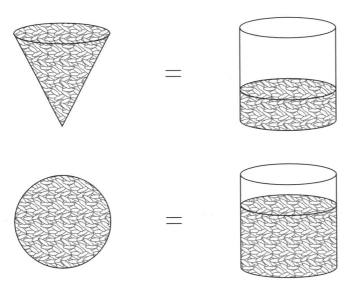

These relationships may also be expressed as follows:

$$\text{volume of the cone} = \tfrac{1}{3}(\text{volume of the cylinder})$$
$$\text{volume of the sphere} = \tfrac{2}{3}(\text{volume of the cylinder})$$

Effects of Changing Attributes

Students also investigate the effects of a change in dimension, surface area, or volume on the other attributes of a three-dimensional object. For example, if 24 unit cubes are arranged in a rectangular shape and packaged in a rectangular box, which arrangement of the cubes will require the least (the most) packaging material? By physically arranging the blocks and determining the surface area of each arrangement, students discover that a column of 24 cubes requires the most packaging, and the arrangement that is the most like a cube (2 by 3 by 4) requires the least amount of packaging. This is similar to ideas students have studied about plane figures: the rectangle that is most like a square has the least perimeter of any rectangle with the same area. (A similar relationship holds for a fixed surface area. The rectangular prism that is the most like a cube will have the greatest volume for a fixed surface area. This relationship is not explored in this unit.)

Through the context of designing an indoor compost box, students also explore the effects that changing a box's dimension has on the volume of the box. Given the dimensions of a compost box known to decompose a half pound of garbage per day, students investigate what size box would decompose one pound of garbage per day. They discover that they need to double only one dimension of a rectangular box to double its volume.

Students also look at the effects of doubling all three dimensions of a box. Making scale models of the original box and the new box helps students visualize the effect of the scale factor. Doubling each dimension of a rectangular prism increases the surface area by $2 \times 2 = 4$ times (a scale factor of 2^2) and volume by $2 \times 2 \times 2 = 8$ times (a scale factor of 2^3). The surface areas of the two prisms, if looked at as flat figures, are similar figures with a scale factor of 2 from the small prism to the large prism. This exploration connects back to ideas in the similarity unit, *Stretching and Shrinking*.

Irregular Objects

Students are introduced to Archimedes'.principle of determining the volume of an object by finding how much liquid it displaces when placed in a container of water. In the process, they also investigate the relationship between milliliters and cubic centimeters.

Measurement

All measurements are approximations. In the work in this unit, this idea will become more apparent than usual. Students' calculations of surface area and volume will often involve an approximation of the number π, and they will often use a calculated amount as a value in a subsequent calculation. Be aware that although students' answers will often differ, many different answers may reflect correct reasoning and correct mathematics.

Mathematical and Problem-Solving Goals

Filling and Wrapping **was created to help students**

- Conceptualize volume as a measure of *filling* an object

- Develop the concept of volumes for prisms and cylinders as stacking layers of unit cubes to fill the object

- Conceptualize surface area as a measure of *wrapping* an object

- Determine that the total number of blocks in a prism is equal to the area of its base multiplied by its height (the volume)

- Discover that strategies for finding the volume and surface area of a rectangular prism will work for any prism

- Explore the relationship of the surface areas of rectangular prisms and cylinders to the total area of a flat pattern needed to wrap the solid

- Discover the relationships among the volumes of cylinders, cones, and spheres

- Apply the strategies for finding the volumes of rectangular prisms and cylinders to designing boxes with given specifications

- Reason about problems involving the surface areas and volumes of rectangular prisms, cylinders, cones, and spheres

- Determine which rectangular prism has the least (greatest) surface area for a fixed volume

- Investigate the effects of varying dimensions of rectangular prisms and cylinders on volume and surface area and vice versa

- Estimate the volume of an irregular shape by measuring the amount of water displaced by the solid

- Understand the relationship between a cubic centimeter and a milliliter

The overall goal of the Connected Mathematics curriculum is to help students develop sound mathematical habits. Through their work in this and other geometry units, students learn important questions to ask themselves about any situation that can be represented and modeled mathematically, such as: *How can the concept of volume as the number of unit cubes be transferred to finding volumes of shapes that are not rectangular? What techniques can be used to relate the surface area of curved surfaces to familiar area concepts? How is the idea of wrapping an object related to the idea of surface area? How is the surface area of an object related to its volume? What techniques can be used to find the volume of an irregular figure? Where do familiar three-dimensional shapes appear in the real world?*

Investigation 1: Building Boxes

Students are introduced to the ideas of volume and surface area through the concepts of *wrapping* and *filling,* building on their knowledge of area and perimeter of two-dimensional figures from the grade 6 *Covering and Surrounding* unit. Rectangular prisms are described by their dimensions: length, width, and height. Students design flat patterns for cubic and rectangular boxes, cut them out, and fold them into boxes. They find the area of flat patterns and discover the association between this area and the surface area of the related box. They are introduced to the concept of volume by determining how many unit cubes it would take to fill particular boxes.

Investigation 2: Designing Packages

Students continue their exploration of surface area and investigate its relationship to volume. *Volume* is defined as the number of unit cubes it takes to fill a rectangular box; *surface area* is defined as the amount of wrapping it takes to enclose a box. This investigation focuses on the surface areas of rectangular prisms. Students are asked to examine the amount of packaging material needed to enclose various arrangements of 24 cubic blocks; they find that a 2 by 3 by 4 arrangement has the least surface area, then generalize their findings to any number of blocks. In the process of solving these problems, students develop strategies for finding the surface area of a rectangular box.

Investigation 3: Finding Volumes of Boxes

Students seek more efficient ways to determine the number of cubes a right prism would hold. They discover that the volume of a box is the number of blocks in the bottom layer multiplied by the number of layers—the area of the base times the height of the prism. (This holds for all prisms.) Students apply their strategy to find the volume of a waste site and how long it will take the residents of a certain city to fill the site. Then, they develop a general strategy for finding the volume of any rectangular prism.

Investigation 4: Cylinders

Students find the volume and surface area of a cylinder by following the same process they used for prisms. First, students estimate the volume of a cylinder by determining how many unit cubes would fill the cylinder. The volume is the area of the base of the cylinder multiplied by its height. The concept of the surface area of a cylinder is developed by having students cut out a flat pattern, think about what the dimensions and surface area of the cylinder made from the pattern will be, and then form the cylinder and determine its volume by finding how many unit cubes would fill it. Then, students design a rectangular box with the same volume as a given cylinder, and they discover that the surface area of the box is greater than the surface area of the cylinder.

Investigation 5: Cones and Spheres

Students compare the volumes of a cone, a sphere, and a cylinder of equal radius and equal height. They construct a transparent plastic cylinder and a clay sphere with the same radius and height. They compress the sphere until it fills the bottom of the cylinder, then compute and compare the volumes of the two shapes. Next, they construct a cone with the same height and radius as the cylinder. They compare the volumes of the two shapes by finding how many cones full of rice or sand it takes to fill the cylinder. In these hands-on activities, students determine how many times the volume of the cone or sphere will fill the cylinder and then look for relationships among the three volumes. (Finding the surface areas of cones and spheres is not considered in this unit.) The investigation ends in an application problem in which students compare the volumes of cones, cylinders, and spheres.

Investigation 6: Scaling Boxes

Students study the effects of changing the dimensions or the volume of a rectangular prism in the context of designing compost containers. They explore two central ideas: How do you build a rectangular container with twice the volume of a given box? What effect does doubling each dimension of a rectangular container have on its volume and surface area? After investigating these questions, students apply their knowledge of similarity and scale factors to rectangular boxes.

Investigation 7: Finding Volumes of Irregular Objects

Students explore how to find the volume of an irregular shape by measuring the amount of liquid it displaces when placed in a container of water. In the process, they look at the relationship between milliliters and cubic centimeters.

The ideas in *Filling and Wrapping* build on and connect to several big ideas in other Connected Mathematics units.

Big Idea	Prior Work	Future Work
understanding, calculating, and estimating the surface area of 3-D figures	understanding, calculating, and estimating the perimeter of 2-D figures (*Covering and Surrounding*)	using surface area of cubes to build understanding of quadratic growth (*Frogs, Fleas, and Painted Cubes*)
understanding, calculating, and estimating the volume of 3-D figures	understanding, calculating, and estimating the area of 2-D figures (*Covering and Surrounding*)	using equations of nonlinear relationships (*Say It with Symbols*)
finding and interpreting the dimensions, surface area, and volume of rectangular prisms	understanding what the dimensions of a figure are (*Shapes and Designs*); finding and interpreting perimeter and area of 2-D figures (*Covering and Surrounding*); studying the structure of 3-D cubic figures (*Ruins of Montarek*)	studying maximum and minimum values and mathematical models (*Thinking with Mathematical Models*); developing counting strategies (*Clever Counting*)
developing strategies for finding the dimensions, surface area, and volume of cylinders, cones, and spheres	studying relationships between triangles, rectangles, and parallelograms; developing strategies for finding the perimeter and area of 2-D figures with straight edges (*Shapes and Designs*; *Covering and Surrounding*)	studying quadratic ($y = ax^2 + bx + c$) and exponential ($y = kx^a$) relationships (*Thinking with Mathematical Models*; *Growing, Growing, Growing*; *Frogs, Fleas, and Painted Cubes*)
scaling 3-D figures	enlarging, shrinking, and distorting 2-D figures (*Stretching and Shrinking*); scaling quantities up and down using ratios and proportions (*Comparing and Scaling*)	studying exponential growth (e.g., $y = kx^2$ and $y = kx^3$) (*Growing, Growing, Growing*; *Frogs, Fleas, and Painted Cubes*; *Data Around Us*)
developing strategies for estimating the surface area and volume of irregular 3-D figures	developing strategies for estimating the perimeter and area of irregular 2-D figures (*Covering and Surrounding*)	developing strategies for making inferences about samples and populations (*Samples and Populations*; *Data Around Us*)

Materials

For students

- Labsheets
- Graphing calculators
- Centimeter cubes (about 30 per group)
- Inch cubes (1 per student)
- Small cardboard boxes (such as gift boxes, paper clip boxes, or jewelry boxes; 1 per pair)
- Small cylindrical cans (such as juice or tuna cans or cardboard rolls from paper towels or wrapping paper; 1 per pair)
- Modeling dough (such as Play-Doh®)
- Sand or rice (about a half cup per group)
- 6-cm to 9-cm strip of transparency film (1 per group)
- Clear plastic containers marked in milliliters (such as graduated cylinders; 1 per group)
- Stones and other irregularly shaped objects
- Angle rulers or compasses (optional)
- Metric rulers
- Centimeter and inch grid paper (provided as blackline masters)
- Two-centimeter grid paper (optional; provided as a blackline master)
- Isometric dot paper (optional, for students' work on some ACE questions; provided as a blackline master)
- Transparent tape
- Glue
- Scissors
- Plain paper

For the teacher

- Transparencies and transparency markers (optional)
- Transparent grids (optional; copy the grids onto transparency film)
- Assorted rectangular boxes and cylinders
- Assorted prisms (triangular, rectangular, pentagonal, hexagonal; optional)
- Assorted spheres, cones, and cylinders, including some with the same height and radius (optional; clear plastic models are available commercially)
- Assorted flat patterns (some with flaps) that can be folded into boxes (many stores have gift boxes that come flat)
- News clippings of local waste-disposal issues (optional)
- Tennis ball container with 3 balls (optional)
- Small items for filling containers (such as dried peas or rice)
- Demonstration compost boxes (real compost boxes or scale models; optional)
- String (optional)

Manipulatives

In the investigations in this unit, students use unit cubes to explore the volumes and surface areas of solids. The ideal set of supplies for this unit would include centimeter cubes and inch cubes. However, the activities in the unit can be done with any size cube. If you have only one size cube, refer to it as a *unit cube*, with a volume of 1 cubic unit. In some activities, you will want to supply students with grid paper that fits the size cube with which they are working; in others, students will be able to model with the cubes and make flat patterns for what they see even if the units do not match. Although centimeter cubes are very helpful for developing the concept of volume of a solid, some students will find making flat patterns for boxes modeled with centimeter cubes difficult because of the size of the cubes. For these students, larger cubes would be helpful.

Students also explore containers of various shapes in this unit. Containers may be collected from school, home, or local businesses. Many different sets of geometric solids are commercially available, including transparent models that help students investigate volume relationships. Dale Seymour Publications carries unit cubes and sets of geometric solids.

Technology

Connected Mathematics was developed with the belief that calculators should always be available and that students should decide when to use them. If your students have access to computers, you may want to let them work with one of the several interesting software programs that help develop the concepts of three-dimensional relationships.

Resources

For more information about composting with worms, you might consult the following book.

Appelhof, Mary. *Worms Eat My Garbage.* Kalamazoo, Mich.: Flower Press, 1993.

Pacing Chart

This pacing chart gives estimates of the class time required for each investigation and assessment piece. Shaded rows indicate opportunities for assessment.

Investigations and Assessments	Class Time
1 Building Boxes	4 days
2 Designing Packages	2 days
3 Finding Volumes of Boxes	3 days
Check-Up 1	$\frac{1}{2}$ day
4 Cylinders	4 days
5 Cones and Spheres	3 days
Check-Up 2	$\frac{1}{2}$ day
6 Scaling Boxes	3 days
Quiz	1 day
7 Finding Volumes of Irregular Objects	1 day
Self-Assessment	Take home
Unit Test	1 day

Filling and Wrapping Vocabulary

The following words and concepts are used in *Filling and Wrapping*. Concepts in the left column are those essential for student understanding of this and future units. The Descriptive Glossary gives descriptions of many of these words.

Essential terms developed in this unit	Terms developed in previous units	Nonessential terms
base	area	right prism
cone	circumference	oblique prism
cube	congruent	
cylinder	dimensions	
edge	height	
face	length	
flat pattern	perimeter	
prism	radius	
rectangular prism	width	
sphere		
surface area		
unit cube		
volume		

Embedded Assessment

Opportunities for informal assessment of student progress are embedded throughout *Filling and Wrapping* in the problems, the ACE questions, and the Mathematical Reflections. Suggestions for observing as students explore and discover mathematical ideas, for probing to guide their progress in developing concepts and skills, and for questioning to determine their level of understanding can be found in the Launch, Explore, or Summarize sections of all investigation problems. Some examples:

- Investigation 4, Problem 4.1 *Launch* (page 45a) suggests a process you can use to assess and extend your students' understanding of the relationship between the volume of a rectangular box and the volume of a cylindrical container.

- Investigation 3, Problem 3.2 *Explore* (page 36c) suggests how you might help students deepen their understanding of the volume of a rectangular prism and how it relates to formulas for calculating volume.

- Investigation 6, Problem 6.3 *Summarize* (page 67e) suggests questions you can ask to assess your students' understanding of the concepts of similarity and scale factor as applied to three-dimensional figures.

ACE Assignments

An ACE (Applications–Connections–Extensions) section appears at the end of each investigation. To help you assign ACE questions, a list of assignment choices is given in the margin next to the reduced student page for each problem. Each list indicates the ACE questions that students should be able to answer after they complete the problem.

Check-Ups

Two check-ups, which may be given after Investigations 3 and 5, are provided for use as quick quizzes or warm-up activities. The check-ups are designed for students to complete individually. You will find the check-ups and their answer keys in the Assessment Resources section.

Partner Quiz

One quiz, which may be given after Investigation 6, is provided with *Filling and Wrapping*. The quiz is designed to be completed by pairs of students with the opportunity for revision based on teacher feedback. You will find the quiz and its answers in the Assessment Resources section. As an alternative to the quiz provided, you can construct your own quiz by combining questions from the Question Bank, this quiz, and unassigned ACE questions.

Question Bank

A Question Bank provides questions you can use for homework, reviews, or quizzes. You will find the Question Bank and its answer key in the Assessment Resources section.

Notebook/Journal

Students should have notebooks to record and organize their work. Notebooks should include student journals and sections for vocabulary, homework, and check-ups. In their journals, students can take notes, solve investigation problems, and record their ideas about Mathematical Reflections questions. Journals should be assessed for completeness rather than correctness; they should be seen as "safe" places where students can try out their thinking. A Notebook Checklist and a Self-Assessment are provided in the Assessment Resources section. The Notebook Checklist helps students organize their notebooks. The Self-Assessment guides students as they review their notebooks to determine which ideas they have mastered and which ideas they still need to work on.

The Unit Test

The final assessment in *Filling and Wrapping* is a unit test, which focuses on finding volumes and surface areas of the basic solids—prisms and cylinders—and one solid that is constructed of a cylinder and a cone.

The Optional Unit Project: The Package Design Contest

Filling and Wrapping also includes an optional unit project, the Package Design Contest. The project gives students an opportunity to apply what they have learned about volume and surface area in a real-world application problem. In the project, a fictitious sporting-goods company is sponsoring a contest for the design of three packages to hold standard table-tennis balls. To enter the contest, students are to submit three package designs and a written explanation of the designs to the company. The blackline master describing the project and a guide for assessing the project are included in the Assessment Resources section. A shortened description of the project appears at the end of the student text.

Introducing Your Students to *Filling and Wrapping*

Introduce the unit by briefly discussing some of the questions posed in the student edition—enough to pique students' interest. Ask the class to discuss the kinds of constraints or issues that someone designing a package to hold a product might have to consider. Students might mention such things as stackability, attractiveness, the amount of product to be put in the package, and the cost of the package.

To get an idea of what knowledge students are bringing to this unit, hold up a box, such as a cereal or a popcorn box, and ask students to estimate the volume of the container (the amount of cereal or popcorn it will hold). What strategies do they use for estimating? What units do they use? Help them begin to think of the amount of cereal, popcorn, and so on that will fill a container as the *volume* of the container.

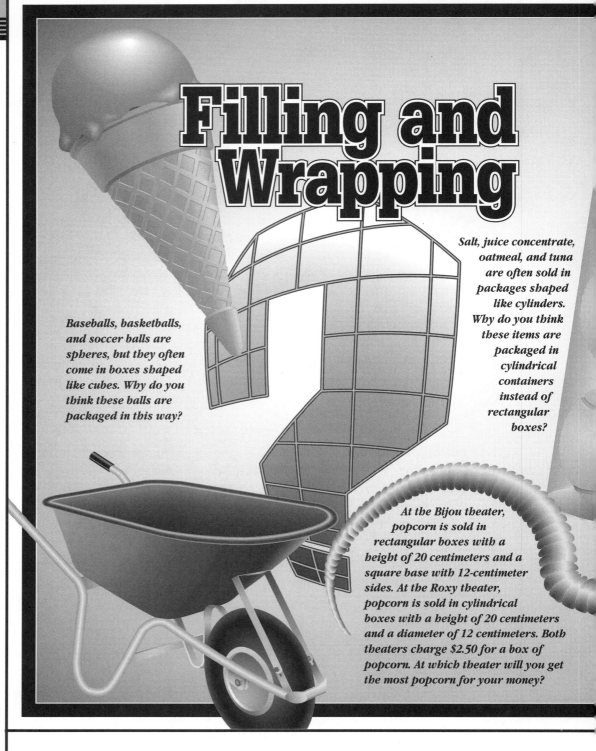

Filling and Wrapping

Baseballs, basketballs, and soccer balls are spheres, but they often come in boxes shaped like cubes. Why do you think these balls are packaged in this way?

Salt, juice concentrate, oatmeal, and tuna are often sold in packages shaped like cylinders. Why do you think these items are packaged in cylindrical containers instead of rectangular boxes?

At the Bijou theater, popcorn is sold in rectangular boxes with a height of 20 centimeters and a square base with 12-centimeter sides. At the Roxy theater, popcorn is sold in cylindrical boxes with a height of 20 centimeters and a diameter of 12 centimeters. Both theaters charge $2.50 for a box of popcorn. At which theater will you get the most popcorn for your money?

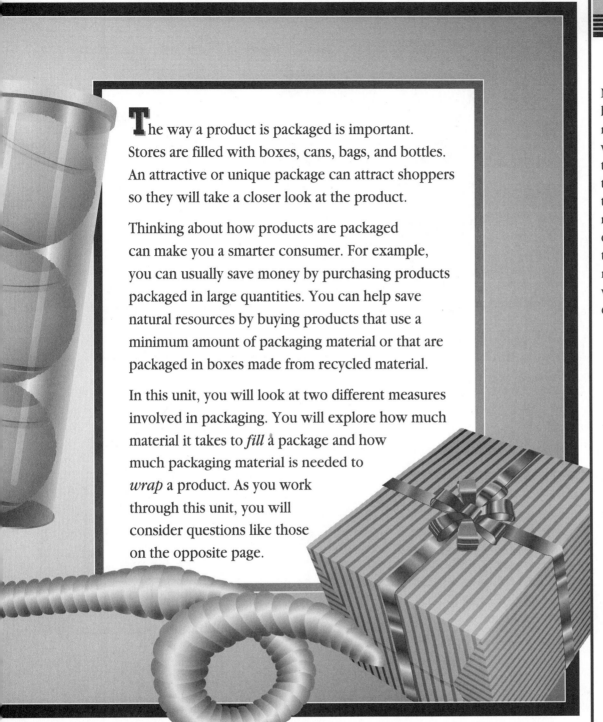

The way a product is packaged is important. Stores are filled with boxes, cans, bags, and bottles. An attractive or unique package can attract shoppers so they will take a closer look at the product.

Thinking about how products are packaged can make you a smarter consumer. For example, you can usually save money by purchasing products packaged in large quantities. You can help save natural resources by buying products that use a minimum amount of packaging material or that are packaged in boxes made from recycled material.

In this unit, you will look at two different measures involved in packaging. You will explore how much material it takes to *fill* a package and how much packaging material is needed to *wrap* a product. As you work through this unit, you will consider questions like those on the opposite page.

Next, ask them to estimate how much material is needed to make the box and why this might be an important question. What units do they use? Ask how they made their estimates and how they might verify them. Help students to connect the idea of the amount of material needed to make a container with the *surface area* of the container.

Mathematical Highlights

The Mathematical Highlights page provides information for students and for parents and other family members. It gives students a preview of the activities and problems in *Filling and Wrapping*. As they work through the unit, students can refer back to the Mathematical Highlights page to review what they have learned and to preview what is still to come. This page also tells students' families what mathematical ideas and activities will be covered as the class works through *Filling and Wrapping*.

Mathematical Highlights

In *Filling and Wrapping*, you will explore important ideas about volume and surface area of three-dimensional objects such as boxes and cans.

● *Filling* containers with unit cubes in a systematic way helps you develop strategies for finding volumes of prisms, cylinders, cones, and spheres.

● Making flat patterns that can be cut out and folded to *wrap* an object helps you develop strategies for finding the surface area of an object.

● Investigating different rectangular arrangements of a set of unit cubes helps you determine which rectangular prisms have the least and greatest surface area for a fixed volume.

● Varying the dimensions of rectangular prisms and cylinders and looking for patterns of change in the volume and surface area leads to some interesting science connections.

● Submerging objects in water helps you develop a strategy for finding volumes of irregular objects.

Using a Calculator

In this unit, you will be able to use your calculator to find areas and volumes of many differently shaped objects. As you work on the Connected Mathematics units, you may decide whether using a calculator will help you solve a problem.

The Investigations

The teaching materials for each investigation consist of three parts: an overview, student pages with teaching outlines, and detailed notes for teaching the investigation.

The overview of each investigation includes brief descriptions of the problems, the mathematical and problem-solving goals of the investigation, and a list of necessary materials.

Essential information for teaching the investigation is provided in the margins around the student pages. The "At a Glance" overviews are brief outlines of the Launch, Explore, and Summarize phases of each problem for reference as you work with the class. To help you assign homework, a list of "Assignment Choices" is provided next to each problem. Wherever space permits, answers to problems, follow-ups, ACE questions, and Mathematical Reflections appear next to the appropriate student pages.

The Teaching the Investigation section follows the student pages and is the heart of the Connected Mathematics curriculum. This section describes in detail the Launch, Explore, and Summarize phases for each problem. It includes all the information needed for teaching, along with suggestions for what you might say at key points in the teaching. Use this section to prepare lessons and as a guide for teaching investigations.

Assessment Resources

The Assessment Resources section contains blackline masters and answer keys for the check-ups, the quiz, the Question Bank, and the Unit Test. Blackline masters for the Notebook Checklist and the Self-Assessment are given. These instruments support student self-evaluation, an important aspect of assessment in the Connected Mathematics curriculum. Discussions of how one teacher assessed students' work on the Unit Test and the Package Design Contest unit project are included, along with sample pages of the students' work.

Blackline Masters

The Blackline Masters section includes masters for all labsheets and transparencies. Blackline masters of centimeter grid paper, two-centimeter grid paper, inch grid paper, and isometric dot paper are also provided.

Additional Practice

Practice pages for each investigation offer additional problems for students who need more practice with the basic concepts developed in the investigations as well as some continual review of earlier concepts.

Descriptive Glossary

The Descriptive Glossary provides descriptions and examples of the key concepts in *Filling and Wrapping*. These descriptions are not intended to be formal definitions but are meant to give you an idea of how students might make sense of these important concepts.

Building Boxes

In this investigation, students are introduced to the ideas of volume and surface area by building on their knowledge of area and perimeter of two-dimensional figures. Students make flat patterns for boxes, cut them out, and fold them into boxes. They find the area of their flat patterns and discover the association between this area and the surface area of the box. Then, they find the volume of a box by filling it with unit cubes.

In Problem 1.1, Making Cubic Boxes, students design flat patterns on grid paper, cut them out, and fold them into unit cubes. The surface area of the cube is the number of grid squares (6 in this case) needed to cover the cube. In Problem 1.2, Making Rectangular Boxes, students make flat patterns for a rectangular box that is not a unit cube. They find the area of each flat pattern (and thus the surface area of the box). They are introduced to the concept of volume by determining how many unit cubes it would take to fill each box. In Problem 1.3, Flattening a Box, they are given a small box and design a flat pattern for it. In Problem 1.4, Testing Flat Patterns, they cut out and fold three flat patterns. For each box they make, they determine the dimensions, the total area of the faces, and the number of cubes needed to fill the box.

Mathematical and Problem-Solving Goals

- *To develop the concept of surface area by counting the number of unit squares needed to wrap (enclose) a rectangular box*

- *To explore the relationship between the surface area of a box and the total area of the unit squares needed to wrap the box*

- *To develop the concept of volume of a rectangular box, and strategies for finding it, by filling a box with unit cubes*

Materials		
Problem	**For students**	**For the teacher**
All	Graphing calculators, inch and centimeter grid paper, metric rulers, scissors, transparent tape, glue	Transparencies 1.1 to 1.4 (optional)
1.3	Small cardboard boxes (such as gift boxes, paper clip boxes, or jewelry boxes; 1 per pair)	Assorted rectangular boxes, and assorted flat patterns (some with flaps) that can be folded into boxes (many stores have gift boxes that come flat)
1.4	Labsheet 1.4 (1 per pair), centimeter cubes (15–20 per pair; or, substitute other unit cubes), and inch cubes (1 per student)	Transparency of Labsheet 1.4 (optional)
1.ACE	Labsheet 1.ACE (optional; 1 per student), grid paper	

INVESTIGATION

Building Boxes

The most common type of package is the rectangular box. Rectangular boxes come filled with everything from cereal to shoes and from pizza to paper clips. Most rectangular boxes begin as flat sheets of cardboard. The sheets are cut and then folded into a box shape and glued or taped together.

1.1 Making Cubic Boxes

Some boxes are shaped like cubes. A **cube** is a three-dimensional shape with six identical square **faces**. What kinds of things might be packaged in cubic boxes?

In this problem, you will make **flat patterns** that can be folded to form boxes. The diagram on the left below shows one possible flat pattern for a cubic box.

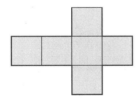 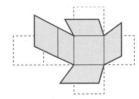

The boxes you will work with in this problem are shaped like unit cubes. A **unit cube** is a cube with **edges** that are 1 unit long. Cubes that are 1 inch on each edge are called inch cubes, and cubes that are 1 centimeter on each edge are called centimeter cubes.

Investigation 1: Building Boxes **5**

Making Cubic Boxes

Launch

- Hold up a cube, and ask the class to describe its features.

- As a class, look at the flat pattern (shown in the student edition) that will cover a unit cube, and talk about its dimensions, perimeter, and area.

- Ask each student to make at least one new pattern.

Explore

- As you circulate, ask students to prove their patterns will work and to compare them.

Summarize

- Have students share the patterns they created, and talk about the area of each.

- Discuss the follow-up questions.

- Do ACE question 16 as a class. *(optional)*

Assignment Choices

ACE questions 1a, 2–5, 9, and 11–16 (1a requires grid paper)

Problem 1.1

A. How many different flat patterns can you make that will fold into a box shaped like a unit cube? Make a sketch of each pattern you find on inch grid paper. Test each pattern by cutting it out and folding it into a box.

B. Find the total area of each pattern.

▓ Problem 1.1 Follow-Up

1. Choose one of your flat patterns from Problem 1.1, and make a copy of it on grid paper. Add the least possible number of flaps you need to be able to fold the pattern and glue it together to make a box with a lid that opens. The lid should have a flap that you tuck in to close the box. On your drawing indicate which flap will be part of the lid and which flaps will be glued. Cut your pattern out and fold it to make sure that it works.

2. Below is Benjamin's work for question 1. Does his pattern meet the requirements given in that question?

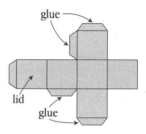

3. Copy Benjamin's flat pattern and add a different set of flaps so that his pattern meets the requirements in question 1.

Answers to Problem 1.1

See page 14g.

Answers to Problem 1.1 Follow-Up

See page 14g.

1.2 Making Rectangular Boxes

Many boxes are not shaped like cubes. The box below has square ends, but the remaining faces are nonsquare rectangles. Next to the box is a flat pattern that could be folded to make the box.

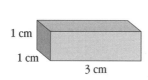

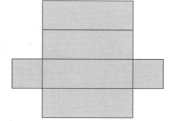

Problem 1.2

A. On grid paper, draw a flat pattern for a rectangular box that is *not* a cube. Each side length of your pattern should be a whole number of units. Then, make a different flat pattern for the same box. Test each pattern by cutting it out and folding it into a box.

B. Find the total area of each flat pattern you made in part A.

C. Describe the faces of the box formed from each flat pattern you made. What are the dimensions of each face?

D. How many unit cubes will fit into the box formed from each flat pattern you made? Explain how you got your answer.

■ Problem 1.2 Follow-Up

Choose one of your flat patterns from Problem 1.2, and make a copy of it on grid paper. Add the least possible number of flaps you need to be able to fold the pattern and glue it together to make a box with a lid that opens. The lid should have a flap that you tuck in to close the box. On your drawing indicate which flap will be part of the lid and which flaps will be glued.

Launch

- Display a rectangular box; ask the class to describe its features; and talk about its faces, edges, and vertices.

- Fold the flat pattern shown in the student edition, and explain that students are to create other patterns to form this rectangular box.

- Have students work individually and then in groups.

Explore

- As you circulate, ask students to prove their patterns will work and to compare their similarities and differences.

Summarize

- Have students share their patterns, and talk about the areas of the patterns and the surface areas of the boxes.

- Discuss the dimensions of a box, and then discuss the follow-up.

Answers to Problem 1.2

A. See page 14h. (Answers for B, C, and D are based on the drawing on page 14h.)

B. The area for each pattern in part A is 14 cm².

C. Four rectangular faces are congruent, with a length of 3 cm and a width of 1 cm. The remaining two faces are also congruent, with a length of 1 cm and a width of 1 cm.

D. 3 unit cubes; One cube will cover the square end and fill one third of the box, so two more will fill the box.

Answer to Problem 1.2 Follow-Up

See page 14h.

Assignment Choices

ACE questions 1b, 8, and unassigned choices from earlier problems (1b and 8 require grid paper)

Flattening a Box

Grouping:
pairs

Launch

- Hold up a box, and talk about its dimensions and what a flat pattern for it might look like.
- Take one measurement of the box, and discuss the number of decimal places students will measure to.
- Demonstrate how to cut the boxes along their edges, and give one box to each pair.

Explore

- Have each student make a pattern for the box and check it with their partner.
- Have pairs cut up their box to match one of the patterns and then work on the follow-up.

Summarize

- Ask students to share their work and any discoveries.
- Talk about the follow-up.
- Introduce the idea of the volumes of the boxes.

Assignment Choices

ACE questions 10, 19, and unassigned choices from earlier problems (19 requires grid paper); also, you may want to have students bring a box from home with its dimensions, the area of its faces, and a pattern for making it

---

1.3 Flattening a Box

A **rectangular prism** is a three-dimensional shape with six rectangular faces. A cube is a special type of rectangular prism. All the boxes you have made so far have been shaped like rectangular prisms. The size of a rectangular prism can be described by giving its dimensions—the length, the width, and the height.

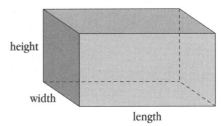

The **base** of a rectangular prism is the face on the bottom, or the face that rests on the table or floor. The length and width of a prism are the length and width of its rectangular base, and the height is the distance from the base of the prism to its top.

Amy is a packaging engineer at the Save-a-Tree packaging company. Mr. Shu asked Amy to come to his class and explain her job to his students. To help the class understand her work, she gave the students boxes and scissors and asked them to do some exploring.

> ### Problem 1.3
>
> Your teacher will give you a box.
>
> **A.** Find the dimensions of your box in centimeters.
>
> **B.** Use the dimensions you found in part A to make a flat pattern for your box on grid paper.
>
> **C.** Cut your box along the edges so that, when you lay it out flat, it will match your flat pattern from part B.

Problem 1.3 Follow-Up

1. Amy explained that one thing she considers when designing a box is the cost of the material. If the material for your box costs $\frac{1}{10}$ of a cent per square centimeter, what is the total cost of the material for your box? Why might this information be useful?

2. What other information or constraints do you think would be important to consider when designing a box?

Answers to Problem 1.3

Answers will vary.

Answers to Problem 1.3 Follow-Up

1. See page 14h.

2. Possible answer: Stores might want to be sure that boxes will fit on shelves in a reasonable way, so the number of objects packed in a box may be considered. The look of a box may be important; for example, does a tall cereal box look like it holds more than a short, squat box? Some materials are better for certain kinds of products than others, and some are easier and more likely to be recycled. Ease in folding the pattern, the amount of material wasted in making the box, the strength of the box, the appeal of the package to the consumer, and shipping considerations may also be important.

1.4 Testing Flat Patterns

The flat patterns below were drawn by one of the engineers at the Save-a-Tree packaging company. The engineer lost his notes that indicated the dimensions of the boxes. Can you help him determine the dimensions?

Box P

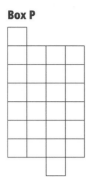

Box Q

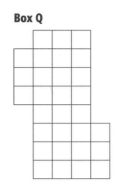

Box R

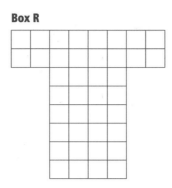

Problem 1.4

A. Cut out each pattern on Labsheet 1.4, and fold it to form a box.

B. Find the dimensions of each box.

C. How are the dimensions of each box related to the dimensions of its faces?

D. Find the total area of all the faces of each box.

E. Fill each box with unit cubes. How many cubes does it take to fill each box?

■ **Problem 1.4 Follow-Up**

Design a flat pattern for a box that has a different shape from box P (from Labsheet 1.4) but that holds the same number of cubes as box P.

Testing Flat Patterns

- - - - - -
At a Glance

Grouping:
pairs

Launch

- Tell the story of the engineer who has lost his notes.

- Distribute Labsheet 1.4 to each pair, and ask students to guess the dimensions of each box before they begin.

Explore

- Have pairs cut out each pattern and find the dimensions of each box and the number of cubes needed to fill it.

- Have pairs work on the follow-up.

Summarize

- Let students talk about how they decided where to fold each pattern.

- Discuss the dimensions of each box, the fact that faces come in pairs, and the number of unit cubes needed to fill each box.

Answers to Problem 1.4

A. See page 14h.

B. *box P:* 1 cm by 1 cm by 6 cm; *box Q:* 1 cm by 3 cm by 3 cm; *box R:* 2 cm by 2 cm by 4 cm

C. The dimensions of each box are from the dimensions of its faces: each combination of two of the three dimensions will yield the dimensions for a pair of congruent faces.

D. *box P:* 26 cm^2; *box Q:* 30 cm^2; *box R:* 40 cm^2

E. *box P:* 6 unit cubes; *box Q:* 9 unit cubes; *box R:* 16 unit cubes

Answer to Problem 1.4 Follow-Up

See page 14i.

Assignment Choices

ACE questions 6, 7, 17, 18, and unassigned choices from earlier problems (you may want to distribute Labsheet 1.ACE for questions 6 and 7)

Answers

Applications

1. See below right.

2. The pattern could not be folded into a closed cube.

3. The pattern could be folded into a closed cube.

4. The pattern could not be folded into a closed cube.

5. The pattern could be folded into a closed cube.

6. Patterns i and ii could be folded to form a closed box; pattern iii could not.

As you work on these ACE questions, use your calculator whenever you need it.

Applications

1. An *open box* is a box without a top.

    a. On grid paper, sketch flat patterns for three different open cubic boxes. Find the area of each flat pattern you found.

    b. On grid paper, sketch flat patterns for three different open rectangular boxes (not cubic boxes) with square ends. Find the area of each flat pattern you found.

In 2–5, tell whether the flat pattern could be folded along the lines to form a closed cubic box. If you are unsure, cut the pattern out of grid paper and experiment.

2.

3.

4.

5.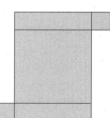

6. Which of these patterns could be folded along the lines to form a closed rectangular box?

i. 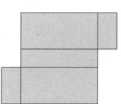   ii.   iii.

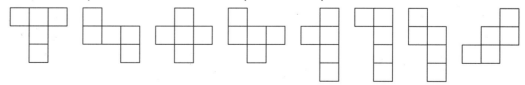

1a. Arrangements of five squares are called *pentominos*. There are 12 pentominos; 8 will fold into an open cube. The area of each pattern is 5 square units.

1b. Possible answer (the areas of these three patterns are 8, 11, and 8 square units):

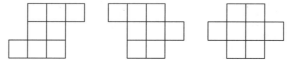

7. Do parts a–c for each pattern from question 6 that forms a box.

a. Use the unit square shown to help you find the dimensions of the box.

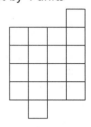

unit square

b. Find the total area of all the faces of the box.

c. Find the number of unit cubes it would take to fill the box.

8. This closed rectangular box does not have square ends.

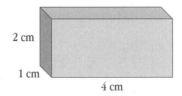

a. What are the dimensions of the box?

b. On grid paper, sketch two flat patterns for the box.

c. Find the area of each flat pattern.

d. Find the total area of all the faces of the box. How does your answer compare to the areas you found in part c?

Connections

9. a. What measurements do you need to find the area and perimeter of a rectangle? Explain how you would use these measurements to find the area and perimeter of a rectangle.

b. What measurements do you need to find the area and perimeter of a square? Explain how you would use these measurements to find the area and perimeter of a square.

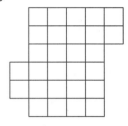

Pattern ii: 1 unit by 2 units by 4 units

7b. *Pattern i:* 18 square units

Pattern ii: 28 square units

7c. *Pattern i:* 4 cubes

Pattern ii: 8 cubes

8. See below left.

Connections

9a. The length and width (also called base and height) are needed. To find the area, multiply the measures together. To find the perimeter, find twice the sum of the length and the width. (Some students may say that the length and width indicate the number of rows and columns of unit squares needed to cover the figure—and thus the area.)

9b. Since all sides of a square are equal, only the measurement of one side is needed. To find the area, multiply this measure by itself. To find the perimeter, multiply this measure by 4.

8a. 4 cm by 1 cm by 2 cm

8b. Possible answer:

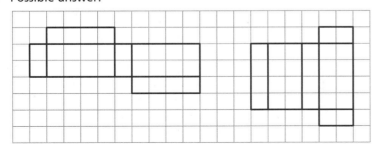

8c. The area of each pattern is 28 square units.

8d. 28 square units; It is the same as the area of each flat pattern.

10a. See below right.

10b. 62 cm²

11. i. 14 units
ii. 14 units
iii. 14 units
iv. 12 units
v. 14 units

12. Hexominos ii and v will fold into a closed box.

13. See page 14i.

14. See page 14i.

15. See page 14i.

---

10. **a.** Draw a flat pattern for a rectangular box with dimensions 2 cm by 3 cm by 5 cm. Find the dimensions and area of each face.

  b. What is the total area of all the faces of the box?

In 11–15, use the following information: A *hexomino* is a shape made of six identical squares connected along their sides. The flat patterns for a closed cubic box are examples of hexominos. Below are five different hexominos.

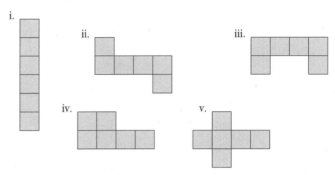

11. Find the perimeter of each hexomino shown above.

12. Which hexominos above could be folded to form a closed cubic box?

13. To which hexominos above can you add one square without changing the perimeter? For each hexomino that works, draw a diagram showing where the square could be added, and explain why the perimeter does not change.

14. To which hexominos above can you add two squares without changing the perimeter? For each hexomino that works, draw a diagram showing where the squares could be added, and explain why the perimeter does not change.

15. To which hexominos above can you add a square that changes the perimeter? For each hexomino that works, draw a diagram showing where the square could be added.

12 **Filling and Wrapping**

10a. Possible pattern:

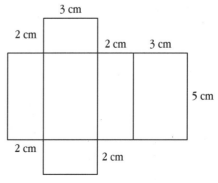

Each face is a rectangle; two are 2 cm by 3 cm (area = 6 cm²); two are 2 cm by 5 cm (area = 10 cm²); and two are 3 cm by 5 cm (area = 15 cm²).

Extensions

16. A number cube is designed so that numbers on opposite sides add to 7. Write the integers from 1 to 6 on one of the flat patterns you found in Problem 1.1 so that it can be folded to form a number cube. You may want to test your pattern by cutting it out and folding it.

17. Could the flat pattern below be folded along the lines to form a rectangular box? If so, explain how.

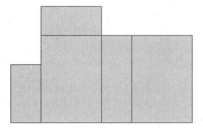

18. Could the flat pattern below be folded along the lines to form an open cubic box? If so, explain how.

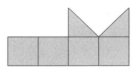

19. Examine the flat patterns you made for cubic boxes in Problem 1.1. Suppose you wanted to make boxes by tracing several copies of the same pattern onto a large sheet of cardboard and cutting them out. Which pattern would allow you to make the greatest number of boxes from a sheet of cardboard? Test your ideas by tiling a piece of grid paper with your box pattern. (*Tiling* is covering a flat surface with copies of a figure with no overlaps or gaps.)

---

16. See below left.

17. This pattern will not fold into a box. The rectangle on the left is not tall enough to match the other faces.

18. This will fold into an open cubic box. Fold the triangle wedges down, and wrap the squares around.

19. Answers will vary. Students should support their answers by showing how the pattern they chose will tile a piece of grid paper.

---

16. Possible pattern:

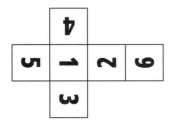

Possible Answers

1. The area of the faces tells the amount of material needed to construct the box, which is important for determining the cost of making the box.

2. The faces of a rectangular box are rectangles. You just need to find the area of each rectangular face and add them. Since every box has three matching pairs of faces, you only need to find the area of the three different faces and then double this total.

3. You can find the number of cubes it would take to fill a box by putting the cubes inside the box and counting how many fit. If the cubes do not fit exactly, you have to estimate the partial cubes that are needed.

4. The number of square units in the flat pattern must be the same. The arrangement of the square units can be different. (Note: Students may have other observations. You might want to discuss students' reflections and test their ideas by examining some of the flat patterns from this investigation.)

In this investigation, you explored rectangular boxes, and you made flat patterns for boxes. You found the dimensions of a box, the total area of all its faces, and the number of unit cubes required to fill it. These questions will help you summarize what you have learned:

1 Suppose you were a packaging engineer. Explain why you might want to know the total area of all the faces of a rectangular box.

2 Explain how you would find the total area of all the faces of a rectangular box.

3 Explain how you would find the number of cubes it would take to fill a rectangular box.

4 What features must be the same for any flat pattern for a given box? What features might be different?

Think about your answers to these questions, discuss your ideas with other students and your teacher, and then write a summary of your findings in your journal.

14 Filling and Wrapping

Tips for the Linguistically Diverse Classroom

Diagram Code The Diagram Code technique is described in detail in *Getting to Know Connected Mathematics*. Students use a minimal number of words and drawings, diagrams, or symbols to respond to questions that require writing. Example: Question 3—A student might answer this question by drawing a stick figure putting cubes into a box and, above the stick figure's head, a thought bubble reading, "12, 13, 14, ..."

TEACHING THE INVESTIGATION

1.1 • Making Cubic Boxes

In this problem, students design flat patterns on grid paper, cut them out, and fold them to form unit cubes. The area of each flat pattern is the surface area of the related cube. This problem helps students see the connection between area of a flat figure and surface area of a solid figure.

Launch

Discuss the work of packaging engineers, who design packages in which to store and ship objects. Packages are often designed under a set of constraints determined by the company and their customers. For example, keeping material use to a minimum is a frequently imposed constraint.

To help students begin thinking about packaging items, read with them the introduction to the investigation in the student edition. Discuss the idea that some boxes are cubes. Read the introduction to Problem 1.1, or ask the class to describe the features of a cube. Students should mention that it has 8 corners or vertices, 12 edges, and 6 faces or sides.

Introduce the term *unit cube.* This is a cube that is used to represent one unit of volume, or one cubic unit. A particular unit cube might be chosen as the basis unit for measuring volume, similar to the decision to measure length in inches or centimeters, or area in square inches or square centimeters. The chosen unit becomes the unit of measurement for a particular situation.

For the Teacher: Using Unit Cubes

In the investigations in this unit, students use unit cubes to explore the volumes and surface areas of solids. The ideal set of supplies for this unit would include centimeter cubes and inch cubes. However, the activities in the unit can be done with any size cube. If you have only one size cube, refer to it as a *unit cube,* with a volume of 1 cubic unit. In some activities, you will want to supply students with grid paper that fits the size cube with which they are working; in others, students will be able to model with the cubes and make flat patterns for what they see even if the units do not match.

In Problem 1.1, students may look at any size cube to construct their pattern for a unit cube on inch grid paper; however, larger cubes are easier to handle.

Make a copy of the flat pattern shown in the student edition, or cut it from Transparency 1.1A and display it on the overhead projector. Use it to review the special features that describe plane figures, such as dimensions, area, and perimeter. Perimeter is the distance around the pattern; area is the number of unit squares in the pattern. Corresponding measures will be developed for three-dimensional figures.

Have students work on the problem in groups of two or three to find other flat patterns that will cover a unit cube. Each student should make at least one new pattern. Assign the follow-up to be done when groups have finished the problem.

Explore

As you circulate, ask students questions about the patterns they are creating.

> How can you prove your patterns will work?
>
> What things are the same in all of the patterns? *(For example, they all have the same area.)* What things are different? *(They are different arrangements of 6 square units of area.)*
>
> How is the area of the pattern related to the number of squares that would be needed to cover the cube?

Summarize

Ask students to display the various patterns on the board or overhead projector. Discuss the patterns that the class generated. Repeat the questions asked in the Explore section above.

Students may argue that some of the patterns are the same (the concept of rotational symmetry is explored in the grade 6 unit *Shapes and Designs*). Two patterns are identical (congruent) if one can be flipped and turned so that it fits exactly on the other figure. For example, the following patterns are all congruent to one another:

Ask the following question to get students thinking about ideas that will later lead to the concept of surface area:

> What is the total area needed to cover a unit cube?

Discuss the follow-up questions. Ask the class to explain their reasoning in question 1 about the number of flaps needed to glue the pattern together. There are 12 edges on any cube, and the 9 edges that are not part of the opening for the lid must have either a fold or a tab for gluing. Each pattern will be constructed of six squares (assuming no partial squares are used) joined together. It will take five folds to join the six squares in a pattern that works, so four tabs must be added somewhere to glue the other edges, and one tab must be added for the lid. If someone has cut out a pattern with flaps, have that student demonstrate it to the class.

You may want to use ACE question 16 as an in-class wrap-up problem.

1.2 • Making Rectangular Boxes

In this problem, students design flat patterns for rectangular boxes.

Launch

Hold up a rectangular box that is not a cube, and ask students to describe it. Discuss the features of the box—faces, edges, and vertices.

> Describe the faces of this rectangular box. *(They are rectangles, and opposite faces are congruent.)* How many faces are there? *(6)*

> How many edges does the box have? *(12)* How many vertices (corners) does it have? *(8)*

> Will a different box have a different number of faces, edges, or vertices?

Hold up a different box. Make sure the class realizes that all rectangular prisms have 6 faces, 12 edges, and 8 vertices.

Explain that packaging engineers may design a rectangular box by drawing a flat pattern that can be cut out and folded to make the box. To model this, use a copy of the flat pattern from the student edition (or cut the pattern from Transparency 1.2A) to form a rectangular box. Explain that the challenge is for students to find other patterns that will fold to form this box. You may want to check that students understand how to find the area of a rectangle. (If they have not worked through the *Covering and Surrounding* unit, you may want to spend a day reviewing the concepts of area and perimeter.)

Distribute inch grid paper, and have students investigate the problem on their own and then compare results in groups of two or three. Assign the follow-up to be done by groups when they have finished the problem.

Explore

Once students have drawn two flat patterns and answered the questions about them, they should gather in their groups to compare their patterns and validate that each can be folded into a rectangular box that is not a cube.

As you circulate, continue to ask questions like those you asked in Problem 1.1. Ask students to prove that their patterns will work; to look for things that are the same in all of the patterns (for example, they have the same area) and things that are different (the various arrangements of the six rectangles); and how the area of each pattern is related to the number of squares that would cover the rectangular box.

Summarize

Give students a chance to share their patterns and prove that they form the correct box. You might want to designate an area for the variety of patterns to be displayed.

Ask students how they found the area of their flat patterns. The relationship between the area of the pattern and the surface area of the related box should arise in the discussion.

What was the area of your flat pattern? How did you find that
measure?

What do you think the total area of the box's surface will be? Why?

How do these areas compare? *(They are the same.)* Why does it make
sense that these two measures are the same?

You want to be sure to help students make the connection between the box's surface area and
the area of plane figures.

You might introduce the upcoming topic of volume by using three cubes, with the same dimensions as the grid paper students are using, to demonstrate how they fill the rectangular boxes. If
three cubes are needed to fill a box, the box has a volume of 3 unit cubes (or 3 cubic units).

Introduce the *dimensions* of a rectangular box: length, width, and height. First, the *base* of the
box must be defined. The length and width of the base are two of the dimensions; the height
of the box is the third. Make sure students are aware that placing the box on a different face
changes the base: the face on the bottom will be called the base.

Give students the dimensions of a new box (preferably one you can display in front of the class),
and ask them to sketch *each* face, labeling the dimensions and area of each face. It is best at this
time to use a box with whole-number dimensions to demonstrate this.

Discuss the follow-up. Have students explain how they reasoned about the number of flaps
needed to glue the pattern together.

How many flaps did you need in the follow-up to Problem 1.1 to glue
the cube pattern together?

Why does it take the same number of flaps to create the rectangular
box as it did to create the cubic box?

1.3 • Flattening a Box

The intent of this problem is to help students understand the relationship between the dimensions
of a box, the faces of a box, and the surface area of a box. Students are to find the dimensions of
a box, then design a flat pattern that will fold into a box with those dimensions.

You will need a small box (such as jewelry boxes, small gift boxes, or individual cereal boxes) for
each pair of students. If you cannot find enough small boxes, tell the students with larger boxes
that each unit on the grid paper corresponds to a particular length on the real box—for example,
1 centimeter on the grid paper might correspond to 5 centimeters on the real box.

The various boxes you have collected may have open tops or tops that overlap. Decide whether
you want students to cut out a pattern that will produce a closed-top or an open-top version of
each box.

Launch

Demonstrate the relationship of the dimensions of a box to the dimensions of its faces. Hold up
one of the boxes.

Can you estimate the length, width, and height of this box? How can we determine these dimensions? *(We can measure them.)* What would a flat pattern for this box look like?

Students should realize that all six faces (five if they are making patterns for open boxes) will be represented in some way in the pattern.

Make one of the measurements, in centimeters, and talk about the fact that it may not be a whole number. Take a couple of minutes to discuss how many decimal places you want students to use in their measurements; tenths should be sufficient.

For the Teacher: Right Rectangular Prisms

In the introduction to Problem 1.3 in the student edition, a rectangular prism is defined as a three-dimensional shape with six rectangular faces. Technically, this defines a *right* rectangular prism. An *oblique* rectangular prism also has opposite sides that are rectangles, but at least two opposite sides must be nonrectangular parallelograms.

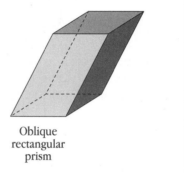

Oblique rectangular prism

Point out to the class that part C of the problem asks them to cut apart the box to match one of their patterns. Demonstrate how to cut a box along its edges. Distribute centimeter grid paper and one box to each pair of students.

Explore

Pairs can work together to measure the faces of their box, but each student should design a pattern for the box. They can exchange and then test their patterns to verify that they fold into a box the same size as the one you have given them.

Some students may need help getting started. Some may need to begin with sketching the individual faces and then assembling them on grid paper to make a connected flat pattern.

Partners will have to decide which pattern they will follow to cut the box, then cut the box to match the selected pattern. (This may be more difficult than it seems. Have tape available for students to use to repair mistakes.) Have pairs move on to the follow-up once they have verified that their patterns work.

Summarize

Let each pair summarize their work and any problems they ran into. The easiest strategy for finding a pattern that works is to think about cutting along the vertical edges and laying the faces of the box flat. Be sure to look for other ways students reasoned about designing a pattern.

Discuss the follow-up questions. Talk about the area of the faces of a box and why this might be an important measurement for a packaging engineer.

You might ask students how many unit cubes will fit into their boxes. If the dimensions of their boxes are not whole numbers, this will require some estimation. Don't talk about rules for finding volume yet; at this point, it is simply the "filling" idea that is important.

1.4 • Testing Flat Patterns

In this problem, students fold boxes from patterns. The area of a flat pattern is the surface area of the related box—the amount of packaging material needed to wrap, or cover, the box. After making the boxes, students fill them with centimeter cubes to find their volumes.

Launch

Tell the story of the engineer who has lost his notes indicating the dimensions of each box. Distribute Labsheet 1.4 to each pair of students. Before students begin cutting out the patterns, ask them to guess and record the dimensions of each box. This will help strengthen their visualization skills.

Explore

Have students cut out the patterns and then find the dimensions and the number of unit cubes needed to fill each box.

Assign the follow-up to be done when they have finished the problem. You might want to ask some students to cut out their patterns to share during the summary.

Summarize

Ask students to explain how they decided where to fold each pattern. Some will have used the symmetry of the two pieces that "stick out" as the place to begin folding.

Discuss the dimensions of each box. Emphasize that the faces of a box come in pairs—this will be an important idea when students develop strategies for finding surface area. Stress the importance of the base, its dimensions, and the height (the distance from the base to the top of the box).

When discussing the number of unit cubes needed to fill each box, *do not go for rules*—it is the filling idea that is important at this stage of students' development of the concept of volume. Some students may have already found effective ways to count the cubes—for example, by multiplying the number of cubes needed to fill the bottom of the box by the number of layers of cubes needed to fill the entire box.

Have students share their solutions to the follow-up. As each student displays his or her pattern and tells the class its dimensions and its area, ask the class whether they agree that the pattern works. Also ask how the pattern, its dimensions, and its area compare to those for box P.

Additional Answers

Answers to Problem 1.1

A. There are 35 different flat patterns that can be made with six squares (these are called *hexominos*). However, only the 11 shown below will fold into a cubic box.

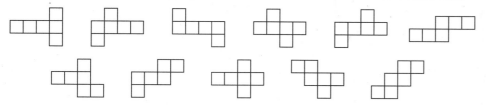

B. The area of each pattern is 6 square units. A unit cube has six faces, each of which has an area of 1 square unit.

Answers to Problem 1.1 Follow-Up

1. Possible answer:

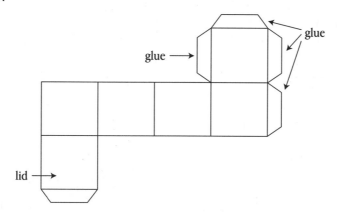

2. The flaps on this pattern won't produce a closed box with a lid; the lid won't open.

3. Possible answer:

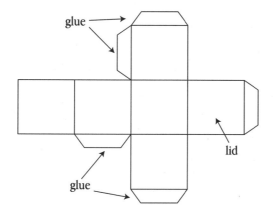

Answers to Problem 1.2

A.   Possible answer:

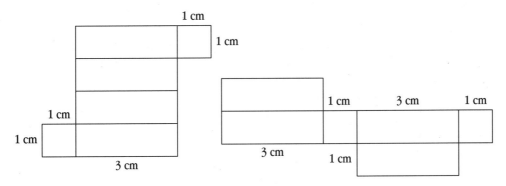

Answer to Problem 1.2 Follow-Up

Possible answer:

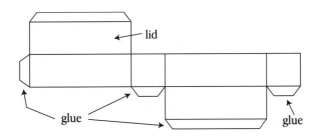

Answers to Problem 1.3 Follow-Up

1.   Answers will vary. For a box of dimensions 3 cm by 1 cm by 1 cm, the total cost of the material is $14 \times \frac{1}{10}$ cent = 1.4 cents. This information would be helpful for determining the total cost of making a given number of boxes.

Answers to Problem 1.4

A.   **Box P**   **Box Q**   **Box R**

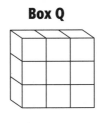
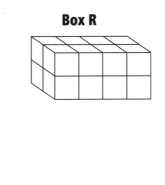

Answer to Problem 1.4 Follow-Up

Box P holds 6 cubes, so any flat pattern that folds into a 1 by 2 by 3 box or a 1 by 1 by 6 box will work. Possible answer:

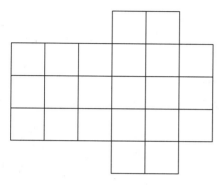

ACE Answers

Connections

13. All the hexominos except hexomino i can have a square added without increasing the perimeter. The perimeter does not change when the square is tucked into a corner—the two units of perimeter that are added cancel the two units that are subtracted. Possible diagram:

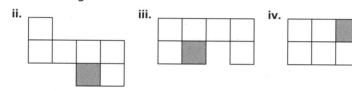

14. Hexominos ii, iv, and v can have two squares added without increasing the perimeter. The perimeter does not change when the squares are placed in two corners. Possible diagram:

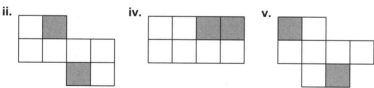

15. All the hexominos can have a square added that changes the perimeter. If one square is added to a noncorner, the perimeter increases by 2. Possible diagram:

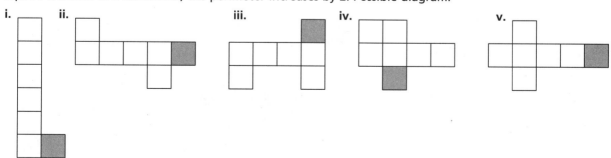

Designing Packages

In this investigation, students continue their exploration of surface area and investigate its relationship to volume.

In Problem 2.1, Packaging Blocks, students investigate surface area in a situation in which volume is fixed by examining the amount of packaging material needed to enclose various arrangements of 24 blocks. In Problem 2.2, Saving Trees, students explore the question of the minimal surface area needed to enclose a rectangular arrangement of any number of cubes. They begin to generalize that, for a fixed volume, the rectangular box that is most like a cube will have the least surface area.

Mathematical and Problem-Solving Goals

- **To develop strategies for finding the surface area of a rectangular box**

- **To determine which rectangular prism has the least (greatest) surface area for a fixed volume**

- **To reason about problems involving surface area**

Materials		
Problem	**For students**	**For the teacher**
All	Graphing calculators, centimeter cubes (about 30 per group; or, substitute other unit cubes)	Transparencies 2.1 to 2.2 (optional)

INVESTIGATION **2**

Designing Packages

Finding the right box for a particular product requires a lot of thought and planning. A company must consider how much a box can hold and the amount and cost of the material needed to make the box.

The amount that a box can hold depends on its volume. The **volume** of a box is the number of unit cubes that would fill the box. The amount of material needed to make or cover a box depends on the box's surface area. The **surface area** of a box is the total area of all of its faces.

The box shown below has dimensions 1 centimeter by 3 centimeters by 1 centimeter. It would take three 1-centimeter cubes to fill this box, so the box has a volume of 3 cubic centimeters. Since it takes fourteen 1-centimeter grid squares to make the box, the box has a surface area of 14 square centimeters.

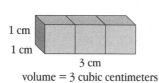

1 cm
1 cm
3 cm
volume = 3 cubic centimeters

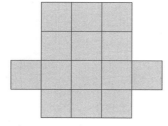

surface area = 14 square centimeters

In this investigation, you will explore the possible surface areas for a rectangular box that holds a given amount. In other words, you will investigate the range of possible surface areas for boxes with a fixed volume.

Packaging Blocks

Launch

- Demonstrate the concepts of volume and surface area.

- Tell the story of the toy company, and as a class explore one arrangement of 24 blocks.

- Have students work on the problem in groups and then do the follow-up individually.

Explore

- Have groups organize their information in a table or in some other way that makes sense to them.

- Help students sketch the arrangements if needed.

Summarize

- Help the class systematically review all of the possible arrangements.

- Discuss patterns in the data.

- Talk about which boxes use the most and least material.

Assignment Choices

ACE questions 1–7, 10, and unassigned choices from earlier problems

---

2.1 **Packaging Blocks**

ABC Toy Company is planning to market a set of children's alphabet blocks. Each block is a cube with 1-inch edges, so each block has a volume of 1 cubic inch.

Problem 2.1

The company wants to arrange 24 blocks in the shape of a rectangular prism and then package them in a box that exactly fits the prism.

A. Find all the ways 24 cubes can be arranged into a rectangular prism. Make a sketch of each arrangement you find, and give its dimensions and surface area. It may help to organize your findings into a table like the one below.

Possible Arrangements of 24 Cubes

Length	Width	Height	Volume	Surface area	Sketch
			24 cubic inches		
			24 cubic inches		
			24 cubic inches		

B. Which of your arrangements requires the least material to make the box? Which requires the most material?

■ **Problem 2.1 Follow-Up**

Which arrangement would you recommend to ABC Toy Company? Write a short report giving your recommendation and explaining the reasons for your choice.

Answers to Problem 2.1

A. See page 23f.

B. The 4 by 3 by 2 box requires the least material. The 24 by 1 by 1 box requires the most material.

Answer to Problem 2.1 Follow–Up

Possible answer: ABC Toy Company should use the 4 by 3 by 2 box because it has the least surface area (52 in²) and would therefore be the least expensive to buy or make. (Note: The box shaped most like a cube will always have the least surface area. This is pursued in more depth in Problem 2.2. Don't expect your class to make this generalization at this time. Some students may argue for boxes based on their visual appeal to the buyer.)

2.2 Saving Trees

Were you surprised to discover that 24 blocks can be packaged in ways that use quite different amounts of packaging material? By reducing the amount of material it uses, a company can save money, reduce waste, and conserve natural resources.

Both boxes have the same volume.

Problem 2.2

When packaging a given number of cubes, which rectangular arrangement uses the least amount of packaging material?

To help you answer this question, you can investigate some special cases and look for a pattern in the results. Explore the possible arrangements of the following numbers of cubes. For each number of cubes, try to find the arrangement that would require the least amount of packaging material.

8 cubes	27 cubes	12 cubes

Use your findings to make a conjecture about the rectangular arrangement of cubes that requires the least packaging material.

Answers to Problem 2.2

The rectangular arrangement of cubes that requires the least packaging material is the arrangement that is most like a cube. For 8 cubes, it is 2 by 2 by 2; for 27 cubes, it is 3 by 3 by 3; and for 12 cubes, it is 2 by 2 by 3.

Saving Trees

At a Glance

Grouping: groups of 3 to 4

Launch

- Review the shape of the box from Problem 2.1 that had the least surface area.
- Introduce the problem of finding what arrangement of cubes will require the least amount of packaging material.
- Have groups work on the problem and follow-up 1 and 2.

Explore

- Encourage groups to try their conjectures on other arrangements and other numbers of cubes.
- Help groups having trouble look at the case of 8 cubes.

Summarize

- Talk about the arrangements students found.
- Help the class think more deeply about the minimal surface area of a rectangular box.
- Use follow-up questions 3 and 4 as a quick assessment.

Assignment Choices

ACE questions 8, 9, 11–13, and unassigned choices from earlier problems

■ Problem 2.2 Follow–Up

1. Test your conjecture from Problem 2.2 on some other examples, such as 30 cubes or 64 cubes. Does your conjecture work for the examples you tried? If not, change your conjecture so it works for any number of cubes. When you have a conjecture that you think is correct, give reasons why you think your conjecture is valid.

2. What rectangular arrangement of cubes uses the most packaging material? Why do you think this is so?

3. What is the surface area of the box below? Explain how you found your answer.

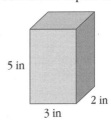

5 in

2 in

3 in

4. Suppose the box in question 3 were resting on a different face. How would this affect its surface area?

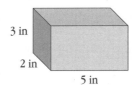

3 in

2 in

5 in

Did you know?

Area is expressed in *square units,* such as square inches or square centimeters. You can abbreviate square units by writing the abbreviation for the unit followed by a raised, or *superscripted,* 2. For example, an abbreviation for square inches is in^2, and an abbreviation for square centimeters is cm^2.

Volume is expressed in *cubic units,* such as cubic inches or cubic centimeters. You can abbreviate cubic units by writing the abbreviation for the unit followed by a superscripted 3. For example, an abbreviation for cubic inches is in^3, and an abbreviation for cubic centimeters is cm^3.

Answers to Problem 2.2 Follow-Up

1. See page 23f.

2. In general, the arrangement with the greatest surface area is the one that is most spread out, so it would require the most packaging material. (Note: This is the 1 by 1 by n arrangement; surface area is maximized because at least four faces of every cube are exposed.)

3. 62 in^2; Possible explanation: The surface area is the sum of the area of the faces. In a rectangular prism, there are three pairs of congruent faces, so you find the area of the three faces and double the sum. In this box, two faces are 5 in by 3 in (15 in^2), two are 3 in by 2 in (6 in^2), and two are 5 in by 2 in (10 in^2); $2(15 + 6 + 10) = 62$ in^2.

4. The surface area of a box is the sum of the area of its six faces and is the same no matter which face is used as the base.

Applications • Connections • Extensions

As you work on these ACE questions, use your calculator whenever you need it.

Applications

In 1–3, a rectangular prism made from inch cubes is pictured. Answer parts a–c.

1.

2.

3.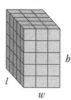

    a. What are the length, width, and height of the prism?

    b. How much material would be needed to make a box for the prism?

    c. How many blocks are in the prism?

4. Suppose you want to make a box to hold exactly thirty 1-inch cubes.

    a. Describe all the possible boxes you could make.

    b. Which box has the least surface area? Which has the greatest surface area?

    c. Why might you want to know the dimensions of the box with the least surface area?

5. a. Sketch a rectangular box with dimensions 2 cm by 3 cm by 6 cm.

    b. What is the surface area of your box?

    c. Sketch a flat pattern for your box. What is the relationship between the area of the flat pattern and the surface area of the box?

Investigation 2: Designing Packages   **19**

5a. Possible sketch:

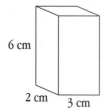

6 cm

2 cm   3 cm

5b. 72 cm²

5c. Possible flat pattern:

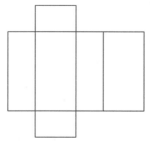

The area of the flat pattern is the same as the surface area of the box.

Answers

Applications

(Note: To find the number of blocks in questions 1–3, some students may count cubes; others may multiply measures. To find the surface area, some students may try to count the faces of the cubes shown; some may add the areas of the faces. What is important at this stage is that they understand that the amount of wrapping is called the *surface area*.)

1a. $l = 5$ in, $w = 3$ in, $h = 1$ in

1b. 46 in²

1c. 15 blocks

2a. $l = 5$ in, $w = 3$ in, $h = 2$ in

2b. 62 in²

2c. 30 blocks

3a. $l = 5$ in, $w = 3$ in, $h = 5$ in

3b. 110 in²

3c. 75 blocks

4a. There are five possible boxes: 1 by 1 by 30, 1 by 2 by 15, 1 by 3 by 10, 1 by 5 by 6, and 2 by 3 by 5.

4b. The 2 by 3 by 5 box has the least surface area, 62 in². The 1 by 1 by 30 box has the greatest surface area, 122 in².

4c. Possible answer: It will cost less to make the box with the least surface area. Also, it might be easier to pack these boxes into a larger box.

5. See left.

Investigation 2   **19**

Connections

6a. See below right.

6b. Other numbers of cubes that can be arranged in only one way to make a rectangular prism are 7, 11, and 13. These are all prime numbers.

7a. See below right.

7b. The 1 by 1 by 10 prism has a surface area of 42 square units; the 1 by 2 by 5 prism has a surface area of 34 square units.

7c. 1 by 2 by 5

7d. Possible answers: 6, 14, 15 (Note: Any number that is the product of two prime numbers has two possible rectangular arrangements. ACE questions 7 and 8 connect to ideas in the grade 6 *Prime Time* unit.)

8. The total area to be painted is 2(150 × 10) + 2(45 × 10) = 3900 ft². About 3900 ÷ 400 = 9.75 or about 10 gallons of paint are needed.

9a. There are 144 in² in 1 ft², so the total area to be painted is 3900 × 144 = 561,600 in². A small can of paint covers 1400 in², so the job will require 561,600 ÷ 1400 ≈ 401.1 or about 402 cans.

9b. Possible answer: the thickness of the coat of paint, the brush or roller used, and whether more than one coat of paint is applied

10. See page 23f.

Connections

6. There is only one way to arrange five identical cubes into the shape of a rectangular prism.

   a. Sketch the rectangular prism made from five identical cubes.

   b. Give some other numbers of cubes that can be arranged into a rectangular prism in only one way. What kind of numbers are these?

7. a. Sketch every rectangular prism that can be made from ten identical cubes.

   b. Find the surface area of each prism you sketched in part a.

   c. Give the dimensions of the prism from part a that has the least surface area.

   d. Find one other number of blocks that has this same number of rectangular arrangements.

8. The dimensions of the recreation center floor are 150 ft by 45 ft, and the walls are 10 ft high. A gallon of paint will cover 400 ft². About how much paint is needed to paint the walls of the recreation center?

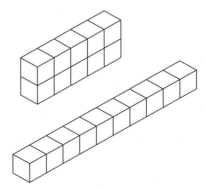

9. a. If a small can of paint will cover 1400 in², about how many cans are needed to paint the walls of the recreation center described in question 8?

   b. What factors might affect how much paint is actually used?

10. a. Graph the relationship between the area of the base and the height for your rectangular arrangements in Problem 2.1.

   b. Describe the relationship between the height and the area of the base.

   c. How might your graph be useful to the packaging engineer at ABC Toys?

6a.

7a.

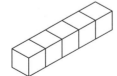

11. The 1994 World Cup soccer championships were held in the United States. Some of the games were played in the Silverdome in Pontiac, Michigan. The dimensions of the soccer field in the Silverdome were 71 m by 115 m.

a. How many square meters of turf were needed to cover the field?

b. What were the dimensions of the field in feet? (1 in = 2.54 cm and 1 m = 100 cm)

11a. $71 \times 115 = 8165$ m^2

11b. $71 \times 100 \times \frac{1}{2.54} \times \frac{1}{12} \approx 233$ ft by $115 \times 100 \times \frac{1}{2.54} \times \frac{1}{12} \approx 377$ ft

Did you know?

The Pontiac Silverdome, like most domed stadiums, normally has a field made from artificial turf. However, the World Cup Soccer Host Committee required that the Silverdome be fitted with a natural grass field that could survive three weeks of soccer matches. The Detroit World Cup Bid Committee asked scientists at Michigan State University to help.

Because of the lack of natural light in the Silverdome, scientists had to design a turf system that could be grown outside the Silverdome and then brought inside and prepared for play. They grew the turf in about 2000 hexagonal pieces, each 7.5 feet wide. About two weeks before the first soccer game was to be played on the turf, the hexagonal pieces were brought inside and pieced together. Why do you think researchers chose hexagons rather than squares, rectangles, or some other shape?

Tips for the Linguistically Diverse Classroom

Rebus Scenario The Rebus Scenario technique is described in detail in *Getting to Know Connected Mathematics.* This technique involves sketching rebuses on the chalkboard that correspond to key words in the story or information that you present orally. Example: Some key words and phrases for which you may need to draw rebuses while discussing the "Did you know?" feature are *soccer* (a soccer ball), *lack of natural light* (darkened dome), *hexagonal pieces* (turf growing in a hexagonal shape), *pieced together* (seven hexagons of turf connected together), *squares* (drawing of squares), *rectangles* (drawing of rectangles), *other shapes* (a diamond, a circle, and a pentagon).

Extensions

12a. A cube-like shape requires less packaging material. The company may have been responding to environmental concerns of consumers. They may also have wanted to change their packaging to get consumers' attention.

12b. The possible arrangements are 1 by 1 by 24, 1 by 2 by 12, 1 by 3 by 8, 1 by 4 by 6, 2 by 2 by 6, and 2 by 3 by 4; dimensions may be width, depth, or height of the box. Possible recommendation: The 1 by 1 by 24 looks like more product but would be quite difficult to carry; the 2 by 2 by 6 may be the easiest to carry, and the 2 by 3 by 4 may save packaging materials.

13a. 1 by 1 by 12, 1 by 2 by 6, 1 by 3 by 4, and 2 by 2 by 3

13b. The surface areas of the boxes above are 50 ft², 40 ft², 38 ft², and 32 ft².

13c. the 2 by 2 by 3 box

13d. Any of the arrangements shown above with *one* of its dimensions doubled will result in a box that would hold 24 basketballs. The one that uses the least amount of material is a 2 by 3 by 4 box, requiring 52 ft² of material, 20 ft² more than the box that requires the least amount of material to hold 12 basketballs.

Extensions

12. Many brands of soft drink are packaged in rectangular boxes of 24 cans.

   a. During the spring of 1993, a major cola company announced that they were going to package 24 cans into a more cube-like shape. Why might the company have done this?

   b. List all the ways 24 cans of soda could be arranged and packaged in a rectangular box. Which arrangement would you recommend that a soft drink company use? Why?

13. Slam Dunk Sporting Goods packages its basketballs in cubic boxes with 1-ft edges.

   a. Slam Dunk ships basketballs from its factory to stores all over the country. To ship the balls, the company packs 12 basketballs (in their boxes) into a large rectangular shipping box. Find the dimensions of every possible shipping box into which the boxes of balls would exactly fit.

   b. Find the surface area of each shipping box you found in part a.

   c. Slam Dunk uses the shipping box that requires the least material. Which shipping box do they use?

   d. Slam Dunk decides to ship basketballs in boxes of 24. They want to use the shipping box that requires the least material. Find the dimensions of the box they should use. How much more packaging material is needed to ship 24 balls than to ship 12 balls?

Mathematical Reflections

In this investigation, you arranged cubes in the shape of rectangular prisms, and you found the arrangements with the least and greatest surface area. These questions will help you summarize what you have learned:

1. For a given number of cubes, what arrangement will give a rectangular prism with the least surface area? What arrangement will give a rectangular prism with the greatest surface area? Use specific examples to illustrate your ideas.

2. Describe how you can find the surface area of a rectangular prism.

Think about your answers to these questions, discuss your ideas with other students and your teacher, and then write a summary of your findings in your journal.

Tips for the Linguistically Diverse Classroom

Original Rebus The Original Rebus technique is described in detail in *Getting to Know Connected Mathematics.* Students make a copy of the text before it is discussed. During the discussion, they generate their own rebuses for words they do not understand; the words are made comprehensible through pictures, objects, or demonstrations. Example: Question 2—Key phrases for which students might make rebuses are *surface area* (rectangular prism in flattened form), *rectangular prism* (sketch of one).

Possible Answers

1. The cube arrangements that give prisms with the greatest surface area are those that are long and thin, and those that give the least surface area are those that are most like cubes. For example, for 36 cubes, a 1 by 1 by 36 arrangement has 146 square units of surface area (the greatest possible); a 3 by 3 by 4 arrangement has 66 square units of surface area (the least possible).

2. The surface area of a rectangular prism is how many square units of area are on all of its faces together. This can be found by adding together the area of each face or by adding the area of three different faces and doubling it (since opposite faces have equal area).

Note: Since opposite faces of a box have equal area, this is really saying that:

Surface area = $2 \times (l \times w) + 2(w \times h) + 2(l \times h)$

or

Surface area = $2 \times (l \times w + w \times h + l \times h)$

However, it is not worth the time to memorize this formula. It is just as quick and easy to find the area of the faces and add them together.

TEACHING THE INVESTIGATION

2.1 • Packaging Blocks

In Investigation 1, students were introduced to the idea of the surface area of a rectangular box and should have begun to make connections between the surface area and the dimensions of a box. In this problem, they find all the possible rectangular arrangements of 24 blocks and the amount of material needed to package them. Students may still be focusing on the area of each face of a box, but they should be using their knowledge about finding the area of a rectangle rather than counting individual squares.

Launch

Use the flat patterns and boxes from Investigation 1 to demonstrate the concepts of volume and surface area. A flat pattern illustrates surface area in a way that students are apt to remember: to find the total surface area, we find the area of each face and add them.

Tell the story of ABC Toy Company. Before they break into groups, ask the class to suggest one arrangement of 24 blocks and discuss how they might find its surface area. If you want students to organize their data in a table (as shown in the student edition), model the process by entering the data about the chosen arrangement into a table. Or, let students decide how to organize their work to look for patterns.

Have students work in groups of two to four. Distribute unit cubes (inch cubes, if you have them) to each group. Assign the follow-up to be done by students on their own as soon as they finish the problem.

Explore

Encourage students to organize their information in a table as suggested in the problem or in some other way that makes sense to them. They should sketch each arrangement they find and label its dimensions.

Visualizing how to sketch the boxes may be difficult for some students. If your students have not studied the grade 6 unit *Ruins of Montarek,* you may want to offer some suggestions for making the sketches. One technique is to think of drawing two offset rectangles, then connecting the corners to form the box.

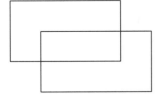 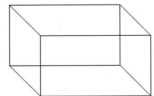 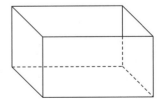

Summarize

Begin the summary by collecting the data students recorded in their tables. You might start with the 24 by 1 by 1 box and model collecting data in an organized manner.

Did anyone find a box that holds exactly 24 cubes and has an edge length of 1? What is the length of the base of this box? What is the width of the base of this box? What is the height of this box?

You know this box has a volume of 24 cubic inches because that was a requirement. How much material will it take to cover this box?

Did anyone find a box that holds exactly 24 cubes and has an edge length of 2? What is the length of the base of this box? What is the width of the base of this box? What is the height of this box?

How much material will it take to cover this box?

Continue with this line of questioning for edge lengths of 3, 4, 5, 6, 7, 8, 12, and 24. Asking for an edge length of 5 or 7 should give rise to a discussion about factors.

You may need to discuss suggested arrangements that are identical; for example, someone may suggest the arrangement with length 2, width 4, and height 3 and another the arrangement with length 4, width 3, and height 2. To demonstrate their equivalence, build the arrangement and set it on the three possible bases. The edges chosen to be length, width, and height are arbitrary, though it is customary to use the length and width of the base as the length and width of the rectangular box.

Students' sketches will vary, depending on which face they use as the base.

How did you decide which face to use for the base? Does your choice affect the surface area of the box? *(no)*

When you have collected all the arrangements that were found, ask students to describe the patterns they see in the table.

Look at the table we have generated. What patterns do you notice? Explain why the patterns make sense.

Here are some patterns students have noticed:

- Chandra: "The volume is always 24 cubic inches." (This is a requirement of the problem.)

- J.J.: "As one dimension increases, another one decreases."

- Pedro: "If you put more cubes in the base, the height decreases because the total is still 24."

- Cie: "Boxes with the same three dimensions have the same volume and surface area; a 1 by 3 by 8 box and an 8 by 3 by 1 box have the same volume and surface area." (They are really the same box oriented differently.)

- Ali: "The product of the length, width, and height must equal 24, which is the volume." (Since length times width tells how many cubes are in a layer, and height tells how many layers there are, multiplying them will give the number of cubes, or cubic inches, that will fill the box.)

Some students will begin to understand that the factors of 24 are what determine the possible arrangements of 24 cubes. Some may see that volume is equal to length × width × height and use this idea to find boxes that work. If students offer the formula for finding the volume of a box, ask them to try the rule on some other boxes—for example, a box with a length of 7 units, a width of 3 units, and a height of 2 units, or a box with a length of 6 units, a width of 8 units, and a height of 1 unit. Ask them to build these boxes and check to see that the pattern for finding the volume works. (If students have not yet discovered this, let it arise in the next problem.)

At this point, students will begin to see that to find the surface area of a prism they need to find the area of each of the six faces and add them. Some will see that opposite faces are equivalent and will double the area of a face to get the area of the pair.

Students may have difficulty when trying to work from the dimensions alone. For example, the surface area of a 2 by 3 by 4 box can be found from this information alone, as each pair of dimensions specifies two faces of the box (2 by 3, 2 by 4, and 3 by 4). Many students will still need to sketch or build the box or make a pattern for it to find the surface area. Asking them to notice opposite faces will move them toward a more efficient process for determining surface area.

Discuss in detail the idea of which box has the least surface area (requires the least amount of material), which has the greatest, and what these boxes look like.

> Which of the boxes with a volume of 24 cubic units has the greatest surface area? *(the 1 by 1 by 24 box)* What does it look like? *(long and skinny)*
>
> Which has the least surface area? *(the 2 by 3 by 4 box)* What does it look like? *(more like a cube)*
>
> If you were going to make a box to hold 36 cubes, which of the possible arrangements of 36 cubes would have the greatest surface area? *(a 1 by 1 by 36 arrangement, with a surface area of 146 square units)* Why? *(Because the cubes are spread out as much as possible.)*
>
> If you were going to make a box to hold 36 cubes, which design would cost you the least to enclose? *(a 3 by 3 by 4 arrangement, with a surface area of 66 square units)* Why? *(Because the cubes are arranged in a more compact fashion, so there is less surface area.)*

Collect students' reports for the follow-up to use as a quick assessment, or have some students read theirs aloud as part of the summary.

2.2 • Saving Trees

This problem encourages students to find a general pattern for which rectangular arrangement of a given number of cubes will have the least surface area. The summary of Problem 2.1 leads nicely into changing the context from looking for a box that will hold exactly 24 cubes to investigating whether there is a way to find the box with minimal surface area regardless of the volume.

Launch

Review what students discovered in Problem 2.1.

> How would you describe the shape of the box we found in the last problem that held 24 cubes and had the least amount of surface area? *(The box was the one in which the dimensions were the closest, 4 by 3 by 2.)*

Introduce Problem 2.2.

> It took a lot of work to find all the possible box arrangements for 24 cubes. From the table we created, we found the box with the least surface area. In mathematics, we are always looking for patterns and rules that will help us to predict outcomes. In today's problem, you are challenged to explore arrangements of different numbers of cubes. You are asked to look carefully at the data and make conjectures about what you think will help you to predict the arrangement that requires the least amount of packaging material.

Let the class work on the problem in groups of three or four.

Explore

Encourage groups who make conjectures about the arrangement of cubes that requires the least amount of packaging material to test other arrangements of the same number of cubes. Also, ask them to test their conjectures on a number of cubes other than the 8, 27, and 12 suggested in the problem.

Groups will have to find a way to organize their data, probably by using a table. If a group is having trouble with the problem, talk through the case of eight cubes with them. Ask them to build each arrangement and to look at the physical objects as well as the measures in their table.

> Look at the dimensions for each arrangement and how they change from one arrangement to another. What is the difference between the box with the greatest surface area and the box with the least surface area?
>
> How does this difference show up in the actual boxes made from cubes?
>
> How does this difference show up in the dimensions of the boxes?

When students in a group complete the problem, have them move on to follow-up questions 1 and 2.

Summarize

Ask students to explain why the more cube-like rectangular arrangement requires the least packaging material.

Describe how you found the amount of packaging material—the surface area—required for the different arrangements you made.

What are the dimensions of the box with the least surface area that holds 8 cubes? The greatest surface area?

Ask the same questions for 27 cubes and 12 cubes. Display the answers to the three questions, putting the boxes with greatest surface area together and those with least surface area together.

How would you describe these shapes compared to these? *(Those with the greatest surface area are long and spread out; those with the least surface area are more compact, more like a cube.)*

Why is the more cube-like rectangular box the box with the least surface area?

Students might answer this by saying something like, "The cube shape hides some squares inside, so their faces do not get counted in the surface area of the cube. In the long 1 by 1 by 27 arrangement, all the cubes have faces exposed; in the 3 by 3 by 3 arrangement, one cube is completely hidden."

Check their understanding by having them describe the dimensions of the box with the least surface area, and then with the greatest surface area, for 100 cubes. Then, help the class further explore the minimal surface area.

For 12 cubes, you found the arrangement with the least surface area to be a 2 by 2 by 3 box. If you could cut the cubes apart, could you package the same volume with even less surface area?

The arrangement with the least surface area for 8 and 27 cubes is a cubic box. The 12-cube arrangement raises the issue of whole-number edges versus fractional-length edges for the minimum surface area.

Students may suggest something like the following: "It's a cube whose dimensions are all the same but when you multiply them together, they equal 30"—in other words, the cube root of the volume. If this comes up, you can use a calculator to guess and check for this number, which is approximately 3.107 or 3.11.

You may want to ask the class to compare the shapes of animals that live in cold climates to those that live in the desert—for example, a polar bear and a snake. Polar bears are more cube-like in that they are designed with a small surface area compared to their volume, which keeps the animals warmer in cold climates. Snakes have a great deal of surface area compared to their volume, which allows heat to escape from their bodies in warm climates.

After the summary, assign follow-up questions 3 and 4 as a quick assessment to see what sense students are making of the ideas in Problem 2.2. Question 3 will tell you whether they have a general strategy for finding the surface area of a box (don't push for symbolic rules).

Additional Answers

Answers to Problem 2.1

A. (Note: Students' sketches may show the same arrangement in a different orientation.)

Possible Arrangements of 24 Cubes

Length (in)	Width (in)	Height (in)	Volume (in³)	Surface area (in²)	Sketch
24	1	1	24	98	
12	2	1	24	76	
8	3	1	24	70	
6	4	1	24	68	
6	2	2	24	56	
4	3	2	24	52	

Answers to Problem 2.2 Follow-Up

1. The most cube-like arrangement requires the least packaging material. For 30 cubes, it is 2 by 3 by 5; for 64 cubes, it is 4 by 4 by 4. Possible explanation: The cube arrangement hides the most faces and entire cubes, and the cubes inside do not have any of their faces exposed.

ACE Answers

Connections

10. The base areas and the heights are given in a table and graph. (Note: Students have to learn that some situations call for inspecting each *different* arrangement, while others require looking at *every* value a variable can have. In this problem, we are interested in every possible value of the base. This forces students to look at the arrangements in more than one way.)

10a.

Area of base (in²)	Height (in)
1	24
2	12
3	8
4	6
6	4
8	3
12	2
24	1

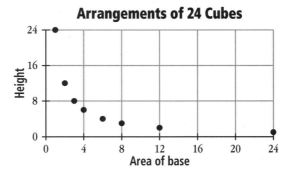

Arrangements of 24 Cubes

10b. As the area of the base increases, height decreases—but not uniformly. That is, as the area decreases by 1, the height changes by a nonconstant amount.

10c. Possible answer: This graph gives the dimensions of all the boxes with a volume of 24 in³—not just those with sides in whole-number amounts. It might also be used to find the approximate base area given a height restriction, or vice versa.

Finding Volumes of Boxes

In Investigation 2, students found strategies for determining the surface area of a rectangular prism, and they found the volume of a box by counting the number of unit cubes it would hold. Now they will seek more efficient ways to determine the number of cubes based on the dimensions of any rectangular prism, including those with a base of another shape. The strategy is the same for all rectangular prisms.

In Problem 3.1, Filling Rectangular Boxes, students imagine filling boxes with 1-inch blocks in a systematic way: placing a layer of blocks on the base and then determining how many layers are needed to fill the box. The volume of the box is thus the number of blocks in the bottom layer multiplied by the number of layers—the area of the base times the height of the prism. In Problem 3.2, Burying Garbage, students apply their knowledge to find the volume of a waste site and how long it will take a city to fill it. In Problem 3.3, Filling Fancy Boxes, students discover that their strategy for finding the volume of a rectangular prism applies to any right prism.

Mathematical and Problem-Solving Goals

- **To develop a strategy for finding the volume of a rectangular prism by filling it with unit cubes, and to recognize that the number of cubes in the bottom layer is equal to the area of the base**

- **To determine that the total number of unit cubes in a rectangular prism is equal to the area of the base times the height (the volume), and to discover that this strategy works for any prism**

- **To learn that the surface area of a prism is the sum of the areas of its faces, and to apply this strategy to any right prism**

- **To reason about problems involving volume and surface area**

Materials		
Problem	For students	For the teacher
All	Graphing calculators	Transparencies 3.1 to 3.3 (optional)
3.1	Centimeter cubes (optional; for students who want to use them), small cardboard boxes (1 per pair)	Transparent grids (optional; copy the grids onto transparency film)
3.2		News clippings of local waste-disposal issues (optional)
3.3	Centimeter grid paper (several sheets per group; provided as a blackline master), transparent tape, metric rulers, plain paper	Examples of triangular, rectangular, pentagonal, and hexagonal prisms (optional), small items for filling prisms (such as dried peas or rice)
ACE	Isometric dot paper	

Filling Rectangular Boxes

Grouping:
pairs

Launch

■ Talk about the ready-made boxes and the toy company's decision.

■ Hold up a box, and ask students for estimates of its volume and how they made their estimates.

■ Have pairs do the problem.

Explore

■ Have cubes on hand for students who want to use them.

■ Suggest that pairs use a table to organize their work. *(optional)*

Summarize

■ Have students share their answers to the problem.

■ Use the follow-up to help lead students to the formula for volume of a prism.

■ As an assessment, have each pair find the dimensions and volume of a small box.

Assignment Choices

ACE questions 1–8, 13, and unassigned choices from earlier problems (13 requires isometric dot paper); Problem 3.2 could also be assigned as homework

INVESTIGATION

Finding Volumes of Boxes

In the last investigation, you started with a fixed number of cubes and explored the various ways you could arrange them to form a rectangular prism. In this investigation, you will start with boxes shaped like rectangular prisms and determine how many unit cubes they will hold.

3.1 Filling Rectangular Boxes

To package its products, a company may have boxes custom-made. However, a company can save money if it buys ready-made boxes. The Save-a-Tree packaging company sells ready-made boxes in several sizes.

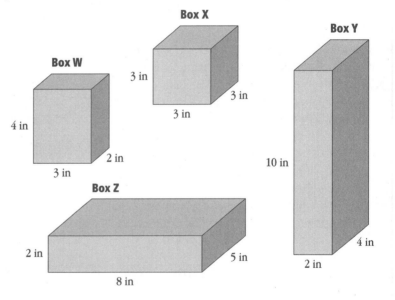

Problem 3.1

ABC Toy Company is considering using one of Save-a-Tree's ready-made boxes to ship their blocks. Each block is a 1-inch cube. ABC needs to know how many blocks will fit into each box and the surface area of each box.

A. How many blocks will fit in each of Save-a-Tree's ready-made boxes? Explain how you got your answer.

B. What is the surface area of each box? Explain how you got your answer.

■ Problem 3.1 Follow-Up

1. How many cubes would fit in a single layer at the bottom of each box in Problem 3.1?

2. How many *identical layers* of cubes could be stacked in each box?

3. The number of unit cubes that fit in a box is the volume of the box. For each box in Problem 3.1, consider the box's dimensions, the number of cubes in a layer, the number of layers, and the volume. What connections do you see among these measurements?

4. Suppose box Y were laid on its side so its base was 4 inches by 10 inches and its height was 2 inches. Would this affect the volume of the box? Explain your reasoning.

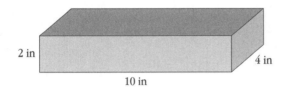

2 in

10 in

4 in

Answers to Problem 3.1

A. *box W:* 24 blocks, *box X:* 27 blocks, *box Y:* 80 blocks, *box Z:* 80 blocks; See the Summarize section for some possible explanations.

B. *box W:* 52 in², *box X:* 54 in², *box Y:* 136 in², *box Z:* 132 in²; See the Summarize section for some possible explanations.

Answers to Problem 3.1 Follow-Up

1. *box W:* 6 cubes, *box X:* 9 cubes, *box Y:* 8 cubes, *box Z:* 40 cubes

2. *box W:* 4 layers, *box X:* 3 layers, *box Y:* 10 layers, *box Z:* 2 layers

3. See page 36f.

4. The volume doesn't change. The number of cubes in the first layer changes but so does the number of layers. The volume is area of the base × height, or 10 × 4 × 2. In the original position, the volume was area of the base × height, or 2 × 4 × 10.

3.2

Burying Garbage

At a Glance

Grouping:
individuals or pairs

Launch

- Assign this problem as home-work, or do it in class.

- Discuss waste-disposal issues.

- Have students work on the problem and follow-up.

Explore

- Encourage students to dis-cuss their strategies with their partners.

- Ask questions about how stu-dents are finding the volume of the site.

Summarize

- Have students share their answers and strategies.

- Ask for estimates on how much garbage would fill the classroom.

- Let students measure the classroom to test their estimates. *(optional)*

The city of Greendale has set aside a piece of land on which to bury its garbage. The city plans to dig a rectangular hole with a base measuring 500 feet by 200 feet and a depth of 75 feet.

The population of Greendale is 100,000. It has been estimated that, on average, a family of four throws away 0.4 cubic foot of compacted garbage a day. How could this information help Greendale evaluate the plan for a waste site?

> **Problem 3.2**
>
> **A.** How much garbage will this site hold?
>
> **B.** How long will it take before the hole is filled?

Problem 3.2 Follow-Up
What suggestions would you make to the Greendale city council about their plan?

3.3 Filling Fancy Boxes

Prisms come in many different shapes. A **prism** is a three-dimensional shape with a top and bottom that are congruent polygons, and faces that are parallelograms. The boxes you have investigated so far in this unit have been shaped like rectangular prisms. A prism is named for the shape of its base. For example, the base of a rectangular prism is a rectangle, and the base of a triangular prism is a triangle. Some prisms are shown below.

   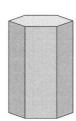

| Triangular prism | Square prism | Pentagonal prism | Hexagonal prism |

Assignment Choices

ACE questions 9, 14–16, and unassigned choices from earlier problems

Answers to Problem 3.2

A. $500 \times 200 \times 75 = 7{,}500{,}000$ ft³ of garbage

B. If the population of 100,000 people is divided into families of four, there are 25,000 families. In one day, these families would throw away $25{,}000 \times 0.4 = 10{,}000$ ft³ of compacted garbage. (Or, one person throws away an average of 0.1 ft³ of compacted garbage, so in one day $100{,}000 \times 0.1 = 10{,}000$ ft³ of garbage is thrown away.) The hole will be filled in $7{,}500{,}000 \div 10{,}000 = 750$ days.

Answer to Problem 3.2 Follow-Up

Possible answer: Because the waste site will last only two years, Greendale will soon be faced with another disposal problem. They may need to build a larger waste site and find ways to cut back on the amount of garbage they produce, such as by composting, insti-tuting recycling programs, and increasing waste-disposal fees.

Filling Fancy Boxes

You have seen that you can find the volume of a rectangular prism by thinking about the number of unit cubes that would fit inside the prism. In this problem, you will see if a similar method will work for finding the volume of a nonrectangular prism. First, you need to make some paper prisms. (These paper prisms are actually prism-shaped boxes that are open at the top and bottom.)

Making paper prisms
- Start with four identical sheets of paper.
- Fold one of the sheets of paper into three congruent rectangles. Tape the paper into the shape of a triangular prism.

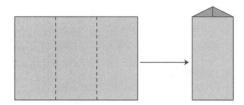

- Fold a second sheet of paper into four congruent rectangles, and tape it into the shape of a square prism.
- Fold and tape the remaining two sheets of paper as shown below to form pentagonal and hexagonal prisms.

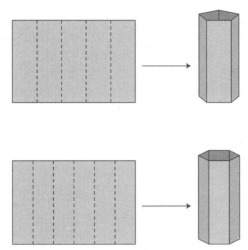

At a Glance

Grouping: small groups

Launch
- As a class, read the information about the various types of prisms.
- Give each group plain paper and centimeter grid paper, tape, and centimeter cubes, and let them work on the problem.

Explore
- Assist students who need help folding the prisms.
- Save the follow-up questions for the summary.

Summarize
- Discuss the answers to the problem.
- Ask students for the strategies they used to find the number of cubes that would fit in the first layer of each prism.
- Discuss the follow-up questions.

Assignment Choices

ACE questions 10–12, 17, 18, and unassigned choices from earlier problems

Assessment

It is appropriate to use Check-Up 1 after this problem.

Investigation 3   27

Problem 3.3

In Problems 3.1 and 3.2, you saw that you could find the volume of a rectangular prism by figuring out how many cubes would fit in a single layer at the bottom of the prism and then figuring out how many layers it would take to fill the prism. Do you think this layering method would work for finding volumes of different types of prisms?

A. Find the volumes of the triangular, square, pentagonal, and hexagonal prisms you made in cubic centimeters. Describe the method you use.

B. Imagine that each of your paper prisms had a top and a bottom. How would you find the surface area of each prism? Which of the four prisms would have the greatest surface area?

Problem 3.3 Follow-Up

1. Do parts a and b for each paper prism you made.
  a. Set the paper prism on its base on a sheet of centimeter grid paper. Trace the prism's base. Look at the centimeter squares inside your tracing. How many cubes would fit in one layer at the bottom of the prism? Consider whole cubes and parts of cubes.
  b. How many layers of centimeter cubes would it take to completely fill the prism?
2. What connections can you make between the area of a prism's base, the height of the prism, and the volume of the prism?
3. Suppose you used the same size sheets of paper to make prisms with 7 sides, 8 sides, 9 sides, and so on. What would happen to the shape of the prism as the number of sides increased? What would happen to the volume of the prism as the number of sides increased?

Save your paper prisms for the next investigation.

Answers to Problem 3.3

See page 36f.

Answers to Problem 3.3 Follow-Up

1. a. Students can estimate the number of cubes that would fit on the bottom layer by counting the squares and estimating partial squares.

   b. The number of layers is equal to the height of the prism.

2. The volume is the area of the base multiplied by the height.

3. As the number of sides increases, the shape of the prism approaches a round cylinder and the volume increases. (Note: For a fixed height, the cylinder will have the greatest volume. Cylinders are investigated in Investigation 4.)

Applications • Connections • Extensions

As you work on these ACE questions, use your calculator whenever you need it.

Applications

In 1–3, a rectangular prism made from inch cubes is pictured. Answer parts a–c.

1.

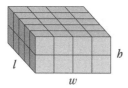

2.

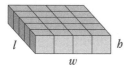

3.

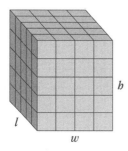

a. What are the length, width, and height of the prism?

b. What is the volume of the prism? Describe how you found the volume.

c. What is the surface area of the prism? Describe how you found the surface area.

Answers

Applications

1a. *l* = 5 in, *w* = 4 in, *h* = 1 in

1b. 20 in³; The volume is the number of blocks in the base times the height, or *l* × *w* × *h*.

1c. 58 in²; The surface area is the sum of the surface area of each face.

2a. *l* = 5 in, *w* = 4 in, *h* = 2 in

2b. 40 in³

2c. 76 in²

3a. *l* = 5 in, *w* = 4 in, *h* = 5 in

3b. 100 in³

3c. 130 in²

5. volume = 32 in³,
surface area = 64 in²

6. volume = 102 in³,
surface area = 145.6 in²

4. **a.** How many cubes are needed to fill the closed box below?

    b. What is the surface area of the box?

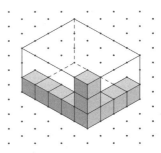

In 5–7, find the volume and surface area of the closed box.

5.

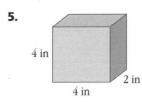

4 in
4 in
2 in

6.

2.5 in
6.8 in
6 in

7.

10 in

4.5 in

1.5 in

8. **a.** Make a sketch of a closed box with dimensions 2 cm by 3 cm by 5 cm.

   b. How many centimeter cubes would fit in one layer at the bottom of the box?

   c. How many layers would be needed to fill the box?

   d. Find the volume of the box.

   e. Find the surface area of the box.

9. Mr. Singh's classroom is 20 ft wide, 30 ft long, and 10 ft high.

   a. Sketch a scale model of Mr. Singh's classroom. Label the dimensions of the classroom on your sketch.

   b. Find the volume of Mr. Singh's classroom. Why might this information be useful to know?

   c. Find the total area of the walls, the floor, and the ceiling. Why might this information be useful to know?

7. volume = 67.5 in³, surface area = 133.5 in²

8a. See below left.

8b. 6 cubes (A different base will produce a different answer.)

8c. 5 layers (A different base will produce a different answer.)

8d. 30 cm³

8e. 62 cm²

9a. See below left.

9b. 6000 ft³; This information would be useful for determining the amount of heat and air conditioning the room requires.

9c. 2200 ft² (including windows and doors); This information would be useful for determining the amount of paint for the walls and ceiling and the amount of carpet or tile for the floor.

8a. Possible sketch:

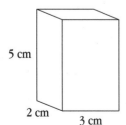

5 cm

2 cm

3 cm

9a.

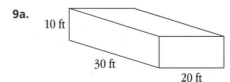

10 ft

30 ft

20 ft

10a. See below right.

10b. 200 cm³

10c. No, not everyone will draw the same prism. Rectangular, triangular, hexagonal, and other prisms—and different versions of each—can be drawn with the given dimensions.

10d. yes; The volume will be the same for every prism with the given dimensions, because the volume is the area of the base multiplied by the height.

11a. 652.5 cubic units; Possible answer: The volume is the area of the base multiplied by the height. You can get the area of the triangle from the rule $\frac{1}{2}$(height × base) or by thinking of it as half of a rectangle:

8.7
10

11b. 537 square units; Possible answer: To find the surface area, you can think of the sides as three 10 by 15 rectangles and add on the areas of the two triangular ends. Or, you can think of the three sides as one large 30 by 15 rectangle and add on the areas of the triangles.

Connections

12. Possible answers: 4 in by 5 in by 4 in (with a surface area of 112 in²); 2.5 in by 8 in by 4 in (with a surface area of 124 in²)

10. **a.** Sketch a prism with a base of area 40 cm² and a height of 5 cm.

b. What is the volume of the prism you drew?

c. Do you think everyone in your class drew the same prism? Explain.

d. Do you think the prisms your classmates drew have the same volume as your prism? Explain.

11. Below are side and top views of a triangular prism with ends that are equilateral triangles.

a. Describe two ways you could find the volume of the prism. What is the volume?

b. Describe two ways you could find the surface area of the prism. What is the surface area?

Side view

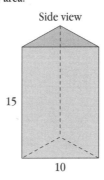

15

10

Top view

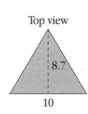

8.7

10

Connections

12. In Problem 3.1, boxes Y and Z have the same volume. Describe the dimensions of another rectangular prism with this same volume but a smaller surface area.

10a. Possible sketch:

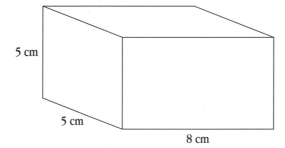

5 cm

5 cm

8 cm

13. a. On isometric dot paper, sketch a closed box with dimensions 4 by 1 by 3.

b. How many unit cubes would fit in a single layer at the bottom of the box you drew?

c. How many layers of unit cubes would be needed to fill the box?

d. Find the volume of the box.

e. Find the surface area of the box.

f. Is there a box with the same volume but less surface area? Explain your answer.

g. Is there a box with the same volume but greater surface area? Explain your answer.

14. The city of Rubberville plans to dig a rectangular landfill. The landfill will have a base with dimensions 700 ft by 200 ft and a depth of 85 ft.

a. How many cubic feet of garbage will the landfill hold?

b. What information would you need to determine how long the landfill can be used until it is full?

c. An excavator was hired to dig the hole for the landfill. How many cubic yards of dirt will he have to haul away?

15. a. Look for an object in your classroom or neighborhood with a volume of about 60 ft³. Explain how you estimated the volume of the object.

b. Look for an object in your classroom or neighborhood with a volume of about 60 cm³. Explain how you estimated the volume of the object.

13a. Possible sketch:

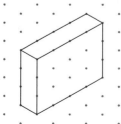

13a. See below left.

13b. 4 cubes (A different base will produce a different answer.)

13c. 3 layers (A different base will produce a different answer.)

13d. 12 cubic units

13e. 38 square units

13f. Yes, a 2 by 2 by 3 box has a surface area of 32 square units. (Note: There are many other boxes with at least one non–whole-number dimension. The cube with sides of length cube root of 12, about 2.289, has the least surface area, about 31.45 cubic units.)

13g. Yes, a 1 by 1 by 12 box has a surface area of 50 square units. (Note: There are many other boxes with at least one non–whole-number dimension. For example, a 0.5 by 0.5 by 48 box has a surface area of 96.5 square units.)

14a. 11,900,000 ft³

14b. You need to know the size of the population and how much garbage, on average, each person produces in a given period of time.

14c. Since there are $3 \times 3 \times 3 = 27$ ft³ in one cubic yard, there are $11,900,000 \div 27 \approx 440,741$ yd³ of dirt.

15. Answers and strategies will vary. Some students may look for objects with shapes similar to a rectangular prism with dimensions that multiply to give 60 ft³ or 60 cm³.

16a. Answers will vary. (Note: If you want to limit this question, you might collect some boxes in advance and let students do this in class. The dimensions, and hence the volume and surface area, will likely be non-integers.)

16b. Answers will vary.

16c. yes; For example, a 1 by 1 by 4 box has a surface area of 18 square units, and a 1 by 2 by 2 box has a surface area of 16 square units; both have a volume of 4 cubic units.

16d. The shape that uses the least packaging material for a fixed volume is a sphere, but spherical-shaped packages are difficult to ship and display. Some manufacturers, however, have started packaging their products in boxes that are more cube-shaped (like some brands of laundry detergent) to use less cardboard.

16e. Students might find it interesting to write or call various companies to ask how they determine package shape and size. An interesting investigation is to compare different sizes of the same product and see which offers the best value per unit of product.

17. See right.

---

16. Find four rectangular boxes in your home.

a. Find the dimensions of each box.

b. Find the volume and surface area of each box.

c. Is it possible for two boxes to have the same volume but different surface areas? Explain why or why not.

d. Why do you think most products are not packaged in the shape that uses the least packaging material?

e. Choose one of the four boxes. See if you can design a box with the same volume as the box you chose but with a smaller surface area. That is, see if you can design a more efficient package.

17. a. Look for objects outside of your classroom that are shaped like prisms. Find three objects that are rectangular prisms and three objects that are nonrectangular prisms.

b. Without measuring, estimate the volume of each object.

c. How could you check the volumes you found in part b?

---

17. Answers and strategies will vary. Some students may estimate volume by comparing the object to one whose volume is known. Some may estimate the dimensions by using a rule of thumb, such as the length of their foot or hand or a floor tile. They might check their answers by measuring the dimensions of the prisms. For nonrectangular prisms, the area of the base may have to be estimated. (Note: You may want to ask students to bring in one of the objects they found so the class can practice estimating volume.)

Extensions

18. The drawing below shows a prism with an odd-shaped top and bottom and rectangular sides. The top and bottom each have an area of 10 cm², and the height is 4 cm. What is the volume of the prism? Explain how you found the volume and why you think your method works.

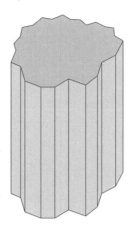

18. 40 cm³; The number of cubes that will fit in one layer is equal to the area of the base, 10 cm². The number of layers that will fit in the prism is equal to its height, 4 cm. The volume is therefore 10 × 4 = 40 cm³.

Possible Answers

1. The number of unit cubes that will fit in one layer of a prism is equal to the area of the base measured in square units. If the prism is a rectangular prism, the number of cubes in one layer is equal to the length of the base times its width. If the base is not a rectangle, you may have to estimate the area of the base. The number of layers is equal to the height of the prism. The total number of cubes that will fill the prism is the volume of the prism and is equal to the number of cubes in one layer times the number of layers.

2. The volume of any prism is the area of the prism's base multiplied by its height.

Mathematical Reflections

In this investigation, you developed methods for finding volumes of rectangular and nonrectangular prisms. These questions will help you summarize what you have learned:

1 What is the relationship between the number of unit cubes needed to fill a prism-shaped box and the volume of the box?

2 Describe how you can find the volume of any prism.

Think about your answers to these questions, discuss your ideas with other students and your teacher, and then write a summary of your findings in your journal.

Tips for the Linguistically Diverse Classroom

Diagram Code The Diagram Code technique is described in detail in *Getting to Know Connected Mathematics*. Students use a minimal number of words and drawings, diagrams, or symbols to respond to questions that require writing. Example: Question 2—A student might answer this question by drawing a prism, labeling its base and height, and writing $b \times h = volume$.

TEACHING THE INVESTIGATION

3.1 • Filling Rectangular Boxes

In this problem, students imagine filling a rectangular prism with unit cubes in whatever way seems reasonable to them. In the follow-up questions, they are helped to think about how to fill the prism systematically. First, they place one layer of cubes on the base. The number of cubes is equal to the area of the base—each cube (or part of a cube) rests on a square (or part of a square) in the base of the prism, so there is a one-to-one correspondence between the number of cubes and the area of the base. Then, they determine how many layers of cubes are needed to fill the box. This is equal to the height of the box. Thus, the volume of the box is the number of cubes in the bottom layer multiplied by the number of layers—the area of the base times the height of the prism.

Launch

Talk about Save-a-Tree's ready-made box sizes and ABC Toy Company's decision. Hold up a box.

> How many unit cubes do you think would fit in my box? How did you make your estimate?

Constructing one or all of the boxes from transparent grids might help students to visualize volume. If you have the time to make them, show them to the class, or distribute one box to each pair of students. Ask students to estimate the volume of each box. Record some of the estimates on the board. Tell the class that the intent of this problem is for them to look for efficient ways to find the volume of a box. If some students claim that they already have a rule for finding the volume of a box (volume $= l \times w \times b$), question them about it.

> What does your rule mean? Why do you think it will work? Will it work for all prisms?

Let pairs work on the problem. Save the follow-up questions to use during the summary. Remind students to save the transparent boxes for the summary.

Explore

Some students may need cubes to simulate filling the boxes.

You may want to suggest that students organize their work in a table. The organization of the following table will help promote the layering strategy for determining volume.

Box	Cubes in a single layer	Number of identical layers	Volume	Surface area (optional)
W				
X				
Y				
Z				

As students make progress in their pairs, ask them how close their estimates of the volume were to the answers they are finding.

Summarize

Discuss the answers to part A. At this point in the unit, two popular strategies for finding the number of blocks that will fill a box are the following:

- "First we found a layer for box W. The base is 2 inches by 3 inches, so it takes 6 cubic inches to form one layer. Then we saw that it would take four of these layers to fill the box."

- "We used layering, but we saw that for box W, 3×2 is the number of blocks in one layer, and $3 \times 2 \times 4$ is the number of blocks in four layers. We think you can just multiply the three dimensions to get the volume of the box."

If some students offer the formula volume $= l \times w \times h$, ask what this means in terms of counting layers. (This formula will only work for rectangular prisms. The strategy of multiplying the area of the base by the height will work for all prisms.)

Talk about the answers to part B. Students may offer these strategies for finding the surface area of a box:

- "We saw that for each box, two faces are the same. So we found the area of each of the three *different* faces and multiplied each one by 2. Then we just added the three numbers."

- "We pictured folding the box Z flat like this:

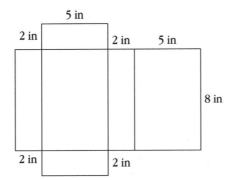

We saw that we had one big rectangle that is 14×8 and two small rectangles that are 2×5. So, the surface area is $14 \times 8 + 2 \times 2 \times 5$."

Use the follow-up questions to help lead students to the formula for volume of a prism. The questions focus students' attention on the bottom layer of a prism and how many layers it will take to fill the prism.

> Why is the number of cubes in the bottom layer equal to the area of the base? (*Each square unit of area can be thought of as the base of a unit cube.*)

If you have constructed models of the boxes, hold one of them up at the orientation shown in the problem.

> Make a sketch of this box while I sketch it at the overhead.

What are the dimensions of the base of this box? What is its height?
What is the volume of the box?

Now, set the box on a different base.

What is the area of the new base? How many cubes will fit on the
base?

How many layers will be needed to fill the box?

Does this new orientation change the volume? Explain your answer.

What is the surface area of this box? Would changing the orientation
of the box change its surface area?

As a quick assessment, give each pair of students a small box, and ask them to find its dimensions and volume. Have them check their answers by filling the box with unit cubes.

3.2 • Burying Garbage

In this problem, students apply their strategy for finding the volume of a rectangular prism to determining the volume of a waste site and how long it will take a certain city to fill it. As the problem involves large numbers, building with cubes is not feasible. Students must look for a way to find the volume using the given dimensions.

As this is a short problem, you may want to assign it as homework rather than exploring it as a class.

Launch

Allow a couple of minutes for students to discuss some of the problems associated with waste disposal. If your community is wrestling with some of these issues, bring in news clippings of the events or discussions.

Have students work individually or in pairs on the problem and follow-up.

Explore

Encourage students to discuss their answers and strategies with their partners.

This problem gives you an opportunity to see whether each student has an understanding of volume. If students are using the strategy of finding the area of the base and multiplying by the height, this shows that they conceptualize volume as a filling or layering process. Ask questions to help them deepen their understanding.

Why is the number of cubes in the bottom layer equal to the area of
the base?

Some students may offer the formula for finding the volume. If so, ask how the formula relates to filling a box with cubes.

Summarize

Go over the answers and strategies that students used in the problem and follow-up.

Ask the class to estimate how much garbage it would take to fill the classroom. If they want to find the exact dimensions of the room, ask that they record their estimates of the room's volume, measure the room, and then evaluate their estimates.

3.3 • Filling Fancy Boxes

In this problem, students discover that their strategy for finding the volume of a rectangular prism applies to any prism.

Launch

As a class, read through the introduction to the various types of rectangular prisms. Hold up a prism that is not rectangular. (If you can't locate one, make a triangular prism by following the directions in the student edition.)

> What do you think the volume of this prism is? How might you find its volume?
>
> How many cubes will fit in the first layer? How would you find out?
>
> How many layers will there be? How would you find out?

In this problem, students are to construct four types of prisms from paper, then find the volume and surface area (assuming they are closed prisms) of each.

> If you are not sure how to find the volumes of these prisms, think about how you found the volumes of rectangular prisms. How are these prisms like rectangular prisms, and how are they different from them?
>
> Make a conjecture about how to find the volume of each prism, and test your conjecture.

Let students work in groups to construct the prisms. Give each group several sheets of plain paper (for constructing the paper prisms; scrap paper would be fine), a few sheets of centimeter grid paper (for setting the prisms on to estimate the volume of the bottom layer), transparent tape, and centimeter cubes. If you have enough cubes and you want students to be able to fill their paper prisms with cubes, have them construct their prisms from quarter sheets of paper rather than whole sheets.

Explore

If students need help folding the pentagonal prism, suggest that they mark off five equal segments on the top and bottom edge of the paper and use the marks to make the folds. Or, suggest that when they fold the paper, they make sure the segments are congruent. (Some will remember the strategies they used to fold fraction strips in the grade 6 units *Bits and Pieces I* and *Bits and Pieces II.*)

To find the number of cubes in the first layer, students can either estimate the area of the base or place cubes on the base and estimate the number of partial cubes needed to complete it. Some may want to be exact and will remember earlier work in the grade 6 *Covering and Surrounding* unit with finding area. Students should know how to find the area of triangles, rectangles, parallelograms, and how to divide other figures into these basic figures.

Save the follow-up questions for the summary.

Summarize

Go over the answers. Check how students found the number of cubes in the first layer. Here are some strategies students have reported:

- Taylor: "We used the formula for the area of a triangle."

- Lindsay: "We enclosed the base in a rectangle and then subtracted the extra area."

- Mei: "We subdivided the area into rectangles and added the area of all the little rectangles."

- Arlo: "We counted the full squares and then estimated the parts of squares."

Students used similar methods to find area in the *Covering and Surrounding* unit. The strategy for finding the number of cubes in a layer and multiplying by the number of layers is a powerful strategy that works for all prisms (and all cylinders).

Discuss the follow-up questions, which specifically address the layering strategy for finding volume.

> How does the volume of a prism change as the number of sides of the base increases?

Students should notice that volume increases as the number of sides of the polygon increases, though the height remains the same. The perimeter of the base also remains the same, but it encloses a greater and greater area as the number of sides increases.

To demonstrate to the class that the volume increases as the number of sides increases, fill the prisms with small items such as dried peas, pasta, rice, or miniature marshmallows. (This is similar to a problem in the *Covering and Surrounding* unit in which students investigated which plane figure of a set perimeter had the greatest area. The circle is the plane figure with the greatest area.) You may want to construct a few more paper prisms to extend this demonstration. Ask how the shape changes as the number of sides of the base polygon increases. (The shape is approaching a cylinder. The cylinder is the shape with the greatest volume.)

Have students save their paper prisms to compare with the cylinders that they will study in the next investigation.

Additional Answers

Answers to Problem 3.1 Follow-Up

3. The volume is the number of unit cubes that can be put in one layer on the bottom of the box multiplied by the number of layers. The number of cubes in one layer is equal to the area of the base, or length × width. The number of layers is equal to the height. So, the volume of a rectangular prism is area of the base × height, or $l \times w \times h$.

Answers to Problem 3.3

A. Answers will depend on the size paper used. Students should recognize that to find the volume of any right prism, they can use the same method they used for a rectangular prism. The volume is the number of cubes that would fit in the bottom layer times the number of layers, or volume = area of base × height.

B. Answers will depend on the size paper used. The surface area is the sum of the areas of the faces—the two congruent polygons and the rectangular sides. The total surface area of the rectangular faces is the same for all the prisms; the area of the base changes. As the number of sides of the base increases, the surface area of the prism increases, so the hexagonal prism has the greatest surface area of the four prisms.

Cilinders

The process for finding the volume and surface area of a cylinder is developed in the same way as it was for prisms.

In Problem 4.1, Filling a Cylinder, students estimate the volume of a cylinder by finding how many unit cubes would fill the cylinder. In Problem 4.2, Making a Cylinder from a Flat Pattern, students cut out a flat pattern, think about what the dimensions and surface area of the cylinder made from the pattern will be, and then form the cylinder and determine its volume by finding out how many unit cubes will fill it. In Problem 4.3, Designing a New Juice Container, students are asked to make a rectangular box with the same volume as a given cylinder, and they discover that the surface area of the box is greater than the surface area of the cylinder. (Note: If students have not worked through the grade 6 *Covering and Surrounding* unit, they will have a difficult time with the area of a circle. You may want to spend a few days reviewing the concepts from that unit on the area and circumference of a circle.)

Mathematical and Problem-Solving Goals

- *To develop strategies for finding the volume and surface area of a cylinder*

- *To compare the process of finding the volumes and surface areas of cylinders and rectangular prisms*

- *To investigate interesting problems involving the volumes and surface areas of cylinders and prisms*

Materials		
Problem	For students	For the teacher
All	Graphing calculators, centimeter grid paper (several sheets per student; provided as a blackline master)	Transparencies 4.1 to 4.3 (optional)
4.1	Plain paper, scissors, transparent tape, metric rulers, centimeter cubes (for students who want them)	Transparent centimeter grid (optional; copy the grid onto transparency film), cylinders and a rectangular prism (for demonstration), small items for filling cylinders (such as dried peas or rice)
4.2	Labsheet 4.2 (1 per student), small cylindrical cans (such as juice or tuna cans or cardboard rolls from paper towels or wrapping paper; 1 per pair), centimeter cubes (for students who want them)	Transparency of Labsheet 4.2 (optional), cylindrical tennis ball container and string (optional)
4.3	Centimeter grid paper (several sheets per student; provided as a blackline master)	Juice box or can (optional)

Student Pages 37–45　　Teaching the Investigation 45a–45h

INVESTIGATION

Cphlinders

So far in this unit, you have studied boxes shaped like prisms. There are many packages and containers that are not shaped like prisms. For example, salt, juice concentrate, oatmeal, and tuna are often sold in packages shaped like cylinders. A cylinder is a three-dimensional shape with a top and bottom that are congruent circles.

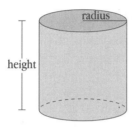

As with a prism, the bottom of a cylinder is called the *base,* and the distance from the base to the top is called the *height.* You can describe a cylinder by giving its dimensions. The *dimensions* of a cylinder are the radius of its base (or top) and its height.

> ### Did you know?
>
> **C**ylindrical cans often contain liquids. The volume, or *capacity,* of containers that hold liquids are often given in units like quarts, gallons, liters, and milliliters. Although volumes given in these units do not tell you how many unit cubes a container will hold, these units are based on cubic measures. For example, a gallon equals 231 cubic inches. In Investigation 7, you will figure out the cubic equivalent of 1 milliliter.

Filling a Cylinder

At a Glance

Grouping: pairs

Launch

- Talk about how to compare the volumes of a cylinder and a rectangular prism.
- Pose the question of how to find the volume of a cylinder without filling it with objects.
- Make a paper cylinder, and ask for volume estimates.
- Have pairs work on the problem and follow-up.

Explore

- If students are having difficulty finding the area of the base, have them place cubes on the grid paper to make a physical model.

Summarize

- Have students share their answers and strategies.
- Talk about units of volume.
- Discuss what measures are needed to define a cylinder.

4.1 Filling a Cylinder

The *volume* of a container is the number of unit cubes it will hold. In the last investigation, you saw that you could find the volume of a prism-shaped box by figuring out how many unit cubes will fit in a single layer at the bottom of the box and then multiplying by the total number of layers needed to fill the box. In this problem, you will develop a method for determining how many cubes will fit inside a cylinder.

> ### Problem 4.1
>
> Make a cylinder by taping together the ends of a sheet of paper. Use the same size paper you used to make the prism shapes in Problem 3.3.
>
> **A.** Set the cylinder on its base on a sheet of centimeter grid paper. Trace the cylinder's base. Look at the centimeter squares inside your tracing. How many cubes would fit in one layer at the bottom of the cylinder? Consider whole cubes and parts of cubes.
>
> **B.** How many layers of cubes would it take to fill the cylinder?
>
>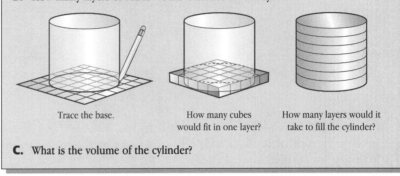
>
> Trace the base.   How many cubes would fit in one layer?   How many layers would it take to fill the cylinder?
>
> **C.** What is the volume of the cylinder?

▨ Problem 4.1 Follow-Up

1. How can you use the dimensions of the cylinder to help you estimate its volume more accurately? Explain.
2. How does the volume of the cylinder compare to the volumes of the prisms you made in Problem 3.3?

Assignment Choices

ACE questions 10, 11, and unassigned choices from earlier problems

Answers to Problem 4.1

A. See page 45g.

B. It would take about 21.6 layers in the first case above and 27.9 in the second.

C. The volume is $62 \times 21.6 \approx 1339$ cm^3 in the first case above, and $37 \times 27.9 \approx 1032$ cm^3 in the second.

Answers to Problem 4.1 Follow-Up

1. You can use the radius of the base to find the area of the base, then multiply by the height.

2. The volume of the cylinder is greater than that of any of the prisms made in Problem 3.3.

4.2 **Making a Cylinder from a Flat Pattern**

In the last problem, you developed a strategy for finding the volume of a cylinder. In this problem, you will develop a strategy for finding the surface area of a cylinder. To do this problem, you will need Labsheet 4.2, which shows a flat pattern for a cylinder.

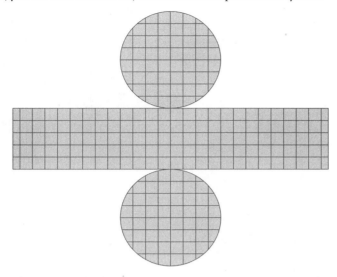

Problem 4.2

Cut out the flat pattern from Labsheet 4.2. Try to cut the pattern so there is a small connector between each circle and the rectangle.

A. What will the dimensions of the cylinder be?

B. What will the surface area of the cylinder be? Explain how you got your answer.

C. Tape the flat pattern together to form a cylinder. How many centimeter cubes will exactly fit in one layer at the bottom of the cylinder? How many cubes will exactly fill the cylinder?

■ Problem 4.2 Follow-Up

1. How are the dimensions of the circles and the rectangle in the flat pattern related to the dimensions of the cylinder?

2. How can you use the dimensions of a cylinder to calculate its volume?

3. How can you use the dimensions of a cylinder to calculate its surface area?

Answers to Problem 4.2

A. The height will be 5 cm, the circumference of each circular end will be 8π or about 25.13 cm, and the radius of each circular end will be 4 cm.

B. about 226 cm²; The surface area of the rectangle is $25.13 \times 5 = 125.7$ cm²; the surface area of each circle is $16\pi = 50.3$ cm²; and $125.7 + 2(50.3) = 226$ cm².

C. The number of cubes that will fit in the bottom layer is equal to the area of the circle, or approximately 50.3 cubes. Five layers of cubes will fit in the cylinder, so $50.3 \times 5 =$ about 251 cubes will fill the cylinder.

Answers to Problem 4.2 Follow-Up

See page 45h.

At a Glance

Grouping: pairs

Launch

■ Distribute small cylinders and have students design flat patterns for them. *(optional)*

■ Have students each make a cylinder from Labsheet 4.2, then work in pairs on the problem and follow-up.

Explore

■ Help students connect features of the flat pattern to those of the cylinder.

Summarize

■ Have students share their ideas about the relationship between the flat pattern and the cylinder, and talk again about finding the surface area and volume of a cylinder.

■ Ask students to design a flat pattern for a cylinder of a given height and radius. *(optional)*

■ Discuss the follow-up.

Assignment Choices

ACE questions 1–4, 6, and unassigned choices from earlier problems

Designing a New Juice Container

**Grouping:
small groups**

Launch

- Talk about the juice company's wish to design a box that holds the same amount of juice as a can.

- Have each student design a box (or, alternatively, bring in a rectangular or cylindrical container and have students design a cylinder or a box with an equivalent volume).

Explore

- Have students work on the problem and follow-up.

Summarize

- Have students share their containers and how they came up with their dimensions.

- Review the follow-up.

- Offer the dimensions of another square box, and ask for the dimensions of a cylinder with the same volume.

Assignment Choices

ACE questions 5, 7–9, 12, 13, and unassigned choices from earlier problems

---

4.3 Designing a New Juice Container

Fruit Tree juice company packages its most popular drink, apple-prune juice, in small cylindrical cans. Each can is 8 centimeters high and has a radius of 2 centimeters.

Recent sales reports indicate that sales of Fruit Tree juice are falling, while sales of juice sold by a competitor, the Wrinkled Prune company, are on the rise. Market researchers at Fruit Tree determine that Wrinkled Prune's success is due to its new rectangular juice boxes. Fruit Tree decides to try packaging their juice in rectangular boxes.

Problem 4.3

Fruit Tree wants the new rectangular box to have the same volume as the current cylindrical can.

A. On centimeter grid paper, make a flat pattern for a box that would hold the same amount of juice as the cylindrical can.

B. Cut out your flat pattern. Use colored pencils or markers to design the outside of the box so it will appeal to potential customers. When you are finished, fold and tape your pattern to form a box.

C. Give the dimensions of your box. Are there other possibilities for the dimensions? Explain.

Problem 4.3 Follow-Up

1. Compare your juice box with the boxes made by your classmates. Which rectangular box shape do you think would make the best juice container? Why?
2. Make a flat pattern for the current cylindrical can.
3. Compare the surface area of the cylindrical can to the surface area of your juice box. Which container has greater surface area?

Answers to Problem 4.3

A. See page 45h.

B. Designs will vary.

C. There are an infinite number of possibilities for the dimensions because there are an infinite number of sets of three numbers with a product of 100.5.

Answers to Problem 4.3 Follow-Up

1. Answers will vary.

2. See page 45h.

3. The surface area of the can is $2(4\pi) + 8 \times 4\pi \approx 125.7$ cm². The surface areas of the boxes will vary, but all will have a greater surface area than the can has. The box with the least surface area is a cube with edges of about 4.65 cm and a surface area of about 130 cm².

As you work on these ACE questions, use your calculator whenever you need it.

Applications

1. A cylindrical storage tank has a radius of 15 ft and a height of 30 ft.

   a. Make a sketch of the tank and label its dimensions.

   b. What is the volume of the tank?

   c. What is the surface area of the tank?

2. A cylinder has a radius of 3 cm. Sand is poured into the cylinder to form a layer 1 cm deep.

   a. What is the volume of sand in the cylinder?

   b. If the height of the cylinder is 20 cm, how many layers of sand—each 1 cm deep—are needed to fill the cylinder?

   c. What is the volume of the cylinder?

3. A soft drink can is a cylinder with a radius of 3 cm and a height of 12 cm. Ms. Doyle's classroom is 6 m wide, 8 m long, and 3 m high. Estimate the number of soft drink cans that would fit inside Ms. Doyle's classroom. Explain how you found your estimate.

Answers

Applications

1a.

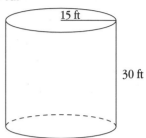

1b. about 21,206 ft³

1c. about 4241 ft²

2a. about 28.3 cm³

2b. 20 layers

2c. about 20 × 28.3 = 566 cm³

3. Answers will vary. One strategy is to find the volume of a carton of 12 or 24 soft drink cans and divide it into an estimate of the volume of the classroom. Another method is to find how many cans fit into a cubic meter and how many cubic meters are in the room and multiply these two numbers together. A soft drink can has a diameter of about 6 cm, so about 16.5 cans in a row will fit along 1 m, or about 272 cans in 1 m². The height of a can is 12 cm, so it would require about 8 layers to fill 1 m³, or about 2176 cans (an underestimate, as cans could be packed tighter than they would be in this array). Filling the room would require at least 144 × 2176 = 313,344 cans.

4a. about 169.6 cm³

4b. about 169.6 cm²

5a. *Open rectangular box:* volume = 2880 cm³, surface area = 1104 cm²; *Open cylindrical box:* volume ≈ 3079 cm³, surface area ≈ 1034 cm²

5b. Possible answer: The container using the least amount of material would cost the least. If customers are willing to pay $2.75 for the amount of popcorn held in the rectangular box, the movie theater would make more money by using the box. To make a better decision, it would be nice to get some potential customers' reactions to the two boxes.

4. Below is a scale model of a flat pattern for a cylinder.

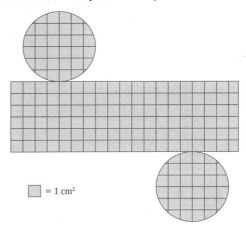

☐ = 1 cm²

a. When the pattern is assembled, what will the volume of the cylinder be?

b. What will the surface area of the cylinder be?

5. You are the manager of a new movie theater. You need to order popcorn boxes, and you must decide between a cylindrical box and a rectangular box. The cylindrical box has a height of 20 cm and a radius of 7 cm, and the rectangular box has a height of 20 cm and a square base with 12-cm sides. The price of each box is based on the amount of material needed to make the box. The theater plans to charge $2.75 for popcorn, regardless of the shape of the box.

a. Find the volume and surface area of each container.

b. Which box would you choose? Give the reasons for your choice. What additional information might help you make a better decision?

Connections

6. How is finding the area of a circle related to finding the volume of a cylinder?

7. Find three different cylindrical objects in your home. For each cylinder, record the dimensions and calculate the volume.

8. A pipeline for carrying oil is 5000 km long and has an inside diameter of 20 cm.

    a. How many cubic centimeters of oil would it take to fill 1 km of the pipeline? (1 km = 100,000 cm)

    b. How many cubic centimeters of oil would it take to fill the entire pipeline?

9. Carlos wants to build a rectangular hot tub that is 4 ft high and holds 1000 ft^3 of water. What could the dimensions of the base of Carlos's hot tub be?

10. The Buy-and-Go Mart sells soft drinks in three sizes. Which size is the best buy? Explain your answer.

12 oz   18 oz   32 oz
$1.25 $1.75 $3.00

11. Tell what features of a cylinder could be measured in the given units.

    a. cm   **b.** cm^2 **c.** cm^3

Connections

6. The ends of a cylinder are circles, and the area of the circular end tells you how many unit cubes would fit in the bottom layer of the cylinder. Multiplying this by the number of layers that would fit in the cylinder (its height) gives the volume.

7. Answers will vary. Typical household objects are cans, paper towel rolls, straws, and cylindrical wastebaskets.

8a. $100\pi \times 100,000 \approx$ 31,416,000 cm^3

8b. about 157,080,000,000 cm^3

9. Dimensions will vary. The base must have an area of 250 ft^2. Possible answers: 12.5 ft by 20 ft; 10 ft by 25 ft

10. The 12-oz drink is about $0.1042 per ounce, the 18-oz drink is about $0.0972 per ounce, and the 32-oz drink is about $0.0938 per ounce. The 32-oz drink is the best buy because it costs the least per ounce.

11a. a length, such as the height, radius, diameter, or circumference of the base

11b. an area, such as the area of the base or the area of the lateral surface

11c. the volume

Extensions

12a. radius = 1 cm, height = 10 cm

12b. 40 cm³ (volume of the box) – 31.4 cm³ (volume of the can) ≈ 8.6 cm³

12c. about $\frac{31.4}{40}$ = 0.785

12d. For any can and box, the volume of the can is $\pi r^2 h$ and the volume of the box is $(2r)^2 h$. The ratio will always be $\frac{\pi r^2 h}{4 r^2 h} = \frac{\pi}{4} \approx 0.785$.

13a. Answers will vary. If students use a standard sheet of paper, the volumes are as follows: With a height of 8.5 in, the circumference of 11 in gives a radius of about 1.75 in. The volume is $\pi \times 1.75^2 \times 8.5 \approx 81.8$ in³. With a height of 11 in, the circumference of 8.5 in gives a radius of about 1.35 in. The volume is $\pi \times 1.35^2 \times 11 \approx 63.0$ in³.

13b. Answers will vary. To see the "cost" of the gain in volume, calculations of surface area must include the top and bottom. If students use a standard sheet of paper, the surface areas are as follows: With a height of 8.5 in, the base area is about 9.62 in², and twice this is 19.24 in². The area of the lateral surface is $8.5 \times 11 = 93.5$ in² for a total of about 112.74 in². With a height of 11 in, the base area is about 5.73 in², and twice this is 11.46 in². The area of the lateral surface is $8.5 \times 11 = 93.5$ in² for a total of about 104.96 in².

Extensions

12. A cylindrical can is packed securely in a box as shown at right. The height of the box is 10 cm, and the sides of its square base measure 2 cm.

    a. Find the radius and height of the can.

    b. What is the volume of the empty space between the can and the box?

    c. Find the ratio of the volume of the can to the volume of the box.

    d. Make up a similar example with a different size can and box. What is the ratio of the volume of the can to the volume of the box for your example? How does the ratio compare to the ratio you got in part c?

13. Start with two identical sheets of paper. Tape the long sides of one sheet together to form a cylinder. Form a cylinder from the second sheet by taping the short sides together. Imagine that each cylinder has a top and a bottom.

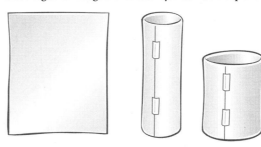

    a. Which cylinder has greater volume? Explain your reasoning.

    b. Which cylinder has greater surface area? Explain your reasoning.

Mathematical Reflections

In this investigation, you developed methods for finding the volume and surface area of a cylinder. These questions will help you summarize what you have learned:

1 Describe how you can find the volume of a cylinder.

2 Describe how you can find the surface area of a cylinder.

3 Discuss the similarities and differences in the methods for finding the volume of a cylinder, a rectangular prism, and a nonrectangular prism.

4 Discuss the similarities and differences in the methods for finding the surface area of a cylinder, a rectangular prism, and a nonrectangular prism.

Think about your answers to these questions, discuss your ideas with other students and your teacher, and then write a summary of your findings in your journal.

Possible Answers

1. The volume of a cylinder can be found by multiplying the number of cubes that would fit in the bottom layer of the cylinder by the number of layers that would fit in the cylinder. Or, it can be found by multiplying the area of the base by the height of the cylinder.

2. The surface area of a cylinder can be found by finding the area of the two circular ends and the area of the lateral surface and adding them together.

3. For prisms and cylinders, the volume is the area of the base times the height. For prisms with bases that are polygons, finding the area depends on what kind of polygon it is. For cylinders, the base is always a circle.

4. For surface area you have to find the areas of all parts of a flat pattern that will cover the prism or cylinder. A cylinder always has a simple flat pattern made up of a square and two circles. Prisms have more faces to worry about.

Tips for the Linguistically Diverse Classroom

Original Rebus The Original Rebus technique is described in detail in *Getting to Know Connected Mathematics*. Students make a copy of the text before it is discussed. During the discussion, they generate their own rebuses for words they do not understand; the words are made comprehensible through pictures, objects, or demonstrations. Example: Question 3—Key words and phrases for which students might make rebuses are *similarities* (two identical circles), *differences* (a shaded circle and an unshaded circle), *volume of a cylinder* (shaded cylinder), *rectangular prism* (shaded rectangular prism), *nonrectangular prism* (shaded triangular prism).

TEACHING THE INVESTIGATION

4.1 • Filling a Cylinder

This problem builds on the ideas developed in Problem 3.3. Students make a cylinder from the same size sheet of paper that they used to construct prisms and develop strategies for finding the volume of a cylinder. In the process, students should see a connection between layering and volume. While circles are more difficult for students to work with than rectangles, the connection to their earlier experiences with layering should give them, by the end of Investigations 3 and 4, a solid understanding that for objects such as prisms and cylinders, volume = area of base × height.

Launch

> **For the Teacher: Useful Models**
>
> Cans and juice-concentrate containers make good models of cylinders. One or two of your sample cylinders should be transparent; look for candy or nut boxes made from clear plastic, borrow some transparent cylindrical beakers from the science teacher, or make some containers from transparency film. Cardboard rolls from paper towels and wrapping paper are easy to cut apart to demonstrate that the lateral surface of a cylinder is a rectangle.
>
> You may also want to obtain (perhaps borrow) a set of manufactured solids. The clear plastic models are particularly useful, as they allow students to work with volume concepts. A cone, sphere, cylinder, cube, and rectangular prism would be particularly helpful.

Hold up a rectangular and cylindrical container that are about the same height and width.

> Which of these two containers will hold more? How can we demonstrate which has the greater volume?

Students' ability to visually estimate volume is probably not well-developed, so it is worth the time to fill one of the containers with rice or some other small item, then pour the rice from one container to the other so students may visually compare the volumes. After the demonstration, discuss with the class other ways of comparing volume and methods for finding the volumes of such containers. Some students may suggest filling each container with rice, sand, or a liquid and then pouring the substance into a measuring cup or beaker.

Hold up one of your sample cylindrical containers—a transparent cylinder if possible—and tell the class its volume, which you have seen on its label or that you have calculated in advance.

> The volume of this container is given on the label as 50 cubic centimeters. What does this number mean?

> We don't want to always have to pour and measure or fill and count to find the volume of a container. Is there a way to find the volume of a cylinder without filling it with cubes or something else?

If students don't bring up what they learned in their work with prisms, drop a few centimeter cubes in the cylinder.

> If I fill this container with centimeter cubes, will that help me find its volume? *(It would give an estimate of the volume but wouldn't be very accurate.)*

Form a cylinder from the same size sheet of paper that students used to make prisms in Problem 3.3. Tape the edge.

> We are going to make cylinders from the same size sheets of paper that we used to make prisms. We will not make a top and bottom, just the lateral surface. When we put the cylinders on our desks, the desks will form the base of the cylinders.

> Before you make your own cylinder, estimate how many centimeter cubes would fill the cylinder I have created. Record your estimate.

> As you work through the problem, keep in mind that in the follow-up you will be asked to figure out how the volume of the cylinder you make compares to the volumes of the prisms that you made in the last investigation.

Distribute plain paper and centimeter grid paper, and let students work in pairs on the problem and follow-up.

Explore

To estimate the area of the base of the cylinder, students can either use the grid paper and count whole and partial squares, or they can use a ruler to measure the radius of the base and calculate the area from the formula for area of a circle. If students have difficulty with the area of a circle, you may want to look at the grade 6 *Covering and Surrounding* unit, especially Investigation 7, for ideas about how to help them build an understanding of why $A = \pi r^2$.

If a group is having trouble, have them draw the outline of the base on grid paper and place centimeter cubes on the squares. Talk about the partial squares that must be covered and counted to find the volume of a single layer of cubes. The illustration in Problem 4.1, in addition to this physical model, should help these students make the connection between the area of the two-dimensional base and the volume of a layer of cubes.

Summarize

Allow students to report and informally discuss the volumes of their cylinders.

> Was your estimate of the cylinder's volume greater than or less than the actual volume? What influenced your estimate?

Draw the base of your paper cylinder on a transparent centimeter grid, and display it on the overhead projector.

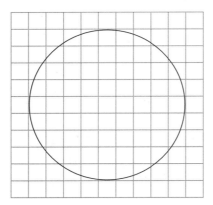

> You found that this is how the base looks when you place your cylinder on grid paper. How did you find the number of cubes in the bottom layer? *(by counting squares or using formulas)*

> How did you use this information to find the volume of your cylinder?

> Suppose we measured the volume of the cylinder using a larger unit cube. How would this affect the number we get for the volume? *(The number would be smaller.)* Suppose we measured the volume using a smaller unit cube. How would this affect the number we get for the volume? *(The number would be greater.)*

> Sometimes we need to measure a cylinder in order to describe it or to compute other measures. What ways can you measure a cylinder so that you can describe it to someone else? *(You can measure the height, the circumference, and the diameter of the base.)*

> How much information would you need to give about a cylinder to be sure that someone else could duplicate the cylinder? *(the height, and one of these three measures: the radius, the diameter, or the circumference of the base)*

> If I give someone the height and volume of my cylinder, would that person be able to make my cylinder?

This is a difficult but interesting question. Using the formula $V = \pi r^2 h$, r can be found from V and h. Let students ponder this question for a few days.

Go over the follow-up questions to see how students thought about them.

4.2 • Making a Cylinder from a Flat Pattern

In this problem, students cut out a flat pattern for a cylinder and explore surface area. In the process, they will make two important discoveries:

■ The circumference of the base of a cylinder is the length of the rectangle that forms the lateral surface of the cylinder.

■ The area of the top of a cylinder (which is the same as the area of the bottom) is the area of a circle, so the area is found more efficiently by measuring the radius of the circular end and applying the formula for area of a circle.

Launch

A great launch activity is to let students struggle with designing a flat pattern for a cylinder before you use the student text or distribute the labsheet; in the problem, students work in the reverse direction, as they are provided with the flat pattern from which to construct a cylinder.

Hold up a cylinder.

> What would a flat pattern for this cylinder look like?

> What information do you need to make a flat pattern for this cylinder? How would you use that information?

Distribute a cylinder (such as juice-concentrate cans or cardboard rolls from paper towels or toilet paper) and grid paper to each pair of students.

> Make whatever measurements you think you need to design a flat pattern that could be used to make a copy of your cylinder.

If students have difficulty, suggest that they start with the base of the cylinder. They can draw around the cylinder to create the circles for the top and bottom. You may have to give them hints about how to draw the lateral surface. They could put a mark on the rim of the cylinder, then roll the cylinder one complete revolution to determine the length of the lateral surface. Some may want to cut out a sheet of paper to wrap around the cylinder, unroll it, and trace around it on their grid paper.

When everyone has successfully constructed a flat pattern for their cylinder, launch the problem.

> On the labsheet I will give you is a flat pattern for another cylinder. You will be working in the reverse direction, making a cylinder from the pattern.

Ask each student to cut the flat pattern from Labsheet 4.2 and then work in pairs to answer the questions in the problem and follow-up.

Explore

As you circulate, ask questions about what students are doing.

> What role does each of these three shapes—the two circles and the rectangle—play in making the cylinder?

> What are the dimensions of the circle? What are the dimensions of the rectangle? How are these dimensions helpful for finding the surface area of the cylinder?

Summarize

Display some of the cylinders the class explored in the launch activity, and let students share their strategies for designing the flat patterns. Then, talk about the flat pattern on the labsheet.

> Can someone describe how this pattern folds into a cylinder? Does this cylinder have only one possible flat pattern?

Students should realize from their experience in the launch that the patterns can look different, but all will contain the same two circles and rectangle.

Ask the class to summarize how to find the surface area of a cylinder. Then, ask them to summarize once again how to find the volume of a cylinder.

To enhance their understanding, you may want to ask students to design a flat pattern for a cylinder with a radius of 2 centimeters and a height of 4 centimeters. They can first determine the circumference and then use the measurements to draw the circles and the rectangle.

For an interesting demonstration that focuses on estimating the height of a circular object, hold up a cylindrical tennis ball container.

> Which is greater: the circumference of this can or its height?

Use a piece of string to demonstrate that the circumference is greater. Students will be surprised.

> Which is greater: the distance around your knee or the distance around your neck?

Have students use their hands to determine the answer. Again, they will probably be surprised.

As a final assessment, you might pose the following question:

> The height of a cylindrical can is 10 centimeters, and the radius of its base is 3 centimeters. Estimate the volume and surface area of the can, remembering that π is a little more than 3. *(First, we need to find the area of the base which is $\pi \times 3^2 = 9\pi$, or about 28 cm². We can use this information to find the volume which is 10 cm × 28 cm, or about 280 cm. The surface area is the sum of the areas of the top and bottom, plus the area of the side. The area of the top equals the area of the bottom, which is 28 cm². The area of the side is the circumference of the base*

times the height. The circumference of the base is $2\pi \times 3$ cm = 6π cm, or about 19 cm. So, the area of the side is 10 cm $\times$ 19 cm, or 190 cm². The total area is therefore 2(28 cm²) + 190 cm², or about 246 cm².)*

The follow-up questions ask about volume and surface area. Students should now see that the surface area of a cylinder can be found by adding the area of the lateral surface to the area of the two circular ends. The area of the lateral surface is the height of the cylinder multiplied by the circumference of the base. The area of each circular end is πr^2. In trying to work from the dimensions of a cylinder to calculate its surface area in follow-up question 3, some students may need to focus on the flat pattern for a given cylinder.

4.3 • Designing a New Juice Container

In this problem, students apply their knowledge of finding volumes and surface areas of cylinders and rectangular prisms.

Launch

Tell the story of how Fruit Tree juice company wants to package individual juice drinks in rectangular boxes with the same volume as the cylindrical cans they are currently using.

> What information will you need to design the rectangular box?
>
> Can we use the same dimensions as the cylinder? Why or why not?

As an alternate way to present the problem, bring in a juice can and ask the class to find its volume and then to design a rectangular container with the same volume. Or, display a rectangular juice container and ask the class to design a cylindrical can with an equivalent volume.

Distribute centimeter grid paper, and have each student design a juice box.

Explore

Allow students time to discuss and design their boxes in small groups. First, they will need to find the volume of the juice can (approximately 100.5 cm³). Ask questions such as the following:

> How do you find the volume of a box? *(area of the base × height)* If you plan for a particular base, how can you find a height to go with it? *(Divide the area of the base into 100.5 to find the number of layers, which equals the height.)*
>
> If I make a base that's 3 centimeters by 4 centimeters, what height would I need? *(about 8.4 centimeters)*

Assign the follow-up to be done as soon as groups have completed their designs.

Summarize

Look for a variety of rectangular boxes. Ask students how they decided on the dimensions of their boxes. Here are some explanations students have offered:

- David: "I decided to make the bottom of the box a 4-centimeter square. So, the area of the base is 16 centimeters. That means the height had to be 100.5 ÷ 16 = about 6.28 centimeters."

- Trisha: "I wanted my box to be 8 centimeters high, just like the can, so the base had to be 100.5 ÷ 8 = 12.6 square centimeters. If one side of the base is 3 centimeters, the other side has to be 12.6 ÷ 3 = 4.2 centimeters."

- Sook Leng: "I found three numbers that multiply to give 100.5, $4 \times 5 \times 5.025 = 100.5$, and made these the dimensions of my box."

Help the class compare the boxes they made.

> Which of these boxes do you think would be easiest to drink from? Which do you think would cost the least to manufacture? Which would be the easiest to pack in a larger shipping box?

Review the follow-up questions.

By this time, students should have a general strategy for finding the volume and surface area of a rectangular prism and of a cylinder. To assess their knowledge, give them a specific problem to work on in class. For example:

> A box of rice has dimensions, in centimeters, of 4 by 16 by 20. What are the dimensions of a cylinder that would hold the same amount of rice?

The volume of the box is 1280 cm^3. If we choose a radius of 5 cm for the cylindrical container, the base will have an area of 78.5 cm^2, so we need a height of 16.3 cm.

> How do the surface areas of the two containers compare?

The surface area of the box is $2(4 \times 16) + 2(4 \times 20) + 2(16 \times 20) = 928$ cm^2. The surface area of the cylinder described above is $2(78.5) + 16.3 \times 31.4 = 669$ cm^2. The cylinder requires about 259 cm^2 less material.

Additional Answers

Answers to Problem 4.1

A. Answers will vary. If students use an 8.5-by-11-inch sheet of paper (21.6 cm by 27.9 cm), with the short side as the height, the radius of the base will be $r = C ÷ 2\pi \approx 4.4$ cm, and the area of the base will be about 62 cm^2. With the long side as the height, the radius of the base will be about 3.4 cm, and the area will be about 37 cm^2.

Answers to Problem 4.2 Follow-Up

1. The radius of the circle is the radius of the base of the cylinder. The circumference of the circle is the length of the rectangle that forms the lateral surface of the cylinder. The width of the rectangle is the height of the cylinder.

2. From the radius of the circle, you can find the area of the base, which tells how many cubes would fit in the bottom layer. Multiply this by the height of the cylinder—which tells how many layers will fit in the cylinder—to get the volume.

3. You can use the radius of the circle to find the surface area of each end, and you can multiply the circumference of the circle by the cylinder's height to find the surface area of the lateral surface. Then, add these surface areas together.

Answers to Problem 4.3

A. Two possible flat patterns:

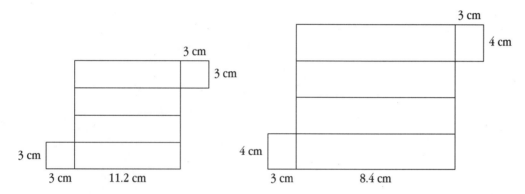

Answers to Problem 4.3 Follow-Up

2.

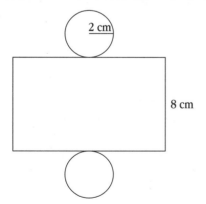

Cones and Spheres

In this investigation, students explore the relationships between the volume of a sphere, the volume of a cone, and the volume of a cylinder. Given a cone, sphere, and cylinder of equal radius and equal height, students conduct experiments to compare the volumes of the cone and sphere to the volume of the cylinder. The strategy suggested in the experiments is to determine how many times the volumes of the cone or sphere will fill the cylinder and then look for relationships among the volumes. (Finding surface areas of cones and spheres is not considered in this unit.)

In Problem 5.1, Comparing Spheres and Cylinders, students construct a transparent plastic cylinder and a clay sphere with the same radius and height. They compress the sphere until it fills the bottom of the cylinder, then compute and compare their volumes. (The volume of the sphere is two thirds the volume of the cylinder.) In Problem 5.2, Comparing Cones and Cylinders, students construct a cone with the same height and radius as the cylinder. They compare the volumes of the two shapes by finding how many cones full of rice or sand it takes to fill the cylinder. (The volume of the cone is one third the volume of the cylinder.) In Problem 5.3, Melting Ice Cream, students compare the volumes of cones, cylinders, and spheres in an application problem.

Mathematical and Problem-Solving Goals

- **To develop strategies for finding the volumes of cones and spheres**

- **To find the relationships among the volumes of cylinders, cones, and spheres**

- **To reason about problems involving cylinders, cones, and spheres**

Materials		
Problem	**For students**	**For the teacher**
All	Graphing calculators	Transparencies 5.1 to 5.3 (optional), assorted spheres, cones, and cylinders, including some with the same height and radius (optional; clear plastic models are available commercially)
5.1	Modeling dough (such as Play-Doh®), 6-cm to 9-cm strips of transparency film (1 strip per group), transparent tape, metric ruler	Cylindrical tennis ball container with 3 balls (optional)
5.2	Sand or rice (about a half cup per group), plain paper, transparent tape, scissors	

Cones and Spheres

Many common and important three-dimensional objects are not shaped like prisms or cylinders. For example, ice cream is often served in *cones*. The planet we live on is very nearly a *sphere*.

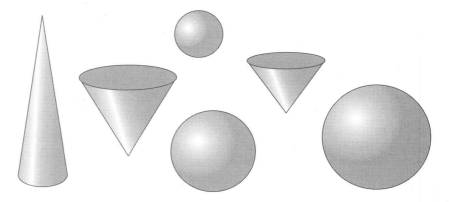

Cones come in many shapes and sizes—from tall and thin to short and wide. As with a cylinder and a prism, we can describe a cone by giving its dimensions. The *dimensions* of a cone are the radius of its circular end and its height.

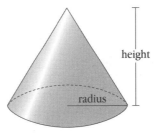

Although spheres may differ in size, they are all the same shape. We can describe a sphere by giving its radius.

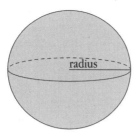

radius

In this investigation, you will explore ways to determine the volume of cones and spheres.

5.1 Comparing Spheres and Cylinders

In this problem, you will make a sphere and a cylinder with the same radius and height and then compare their volumes. (The "height" of a sphere is just its diameter.) You can use the relationship you observe to help you develop a method for finding the volume of a sphere.

Did you know?

The Earth is nearly a sphere. You may have heard that, until Christopher Columbus's voyage in 1492, most people believed the Earth was flat. Actually, as early as the fourth century B.C., scientists in Greece and Egypt had figured out that the Earth was round. They observed the shadow of the Earth as it passed across the Moon during a lunar eclipse. It was clear that the shadow was round. Combining this observation with evidence gathered from observing constellations, these scientists concluded that the Earth was indeed spherical. In fact, in the third century B.C., Eratosthenes, a scientist from Alexandria, Egypt, was actually able to estimate the circumference of the Earth.

Investigation 5: Cones and Spheres 47

Tips for the Linguistically Diverse Classroom

Rebus Scenario The Rebus Scenario technique is described in detail in *Getting to Know Connected Mathematics.* This technique involves sketching rebuses on the chalkboard that correspond to key words in the story or information that you present orally. Example: Some key words and phrases for which you may need to draw rebuses while discussing the "Did you know?" feature are *Earth* (sphere with outline of continents), *shadow* (shadow drawn out from Earth), *Moon during a lunar eclipse* (drawing of Moon with a round shadow on it), *constellations* (stars), *circumference* (line drawn about Earth).

Comparing Spheres and Cylinders

At a Glance

Grouping: whole class or small groups

Launch

- Hold up a cylinder and a sphere of similar diameter, and ask students how their volumes compare.
- Talk about the experiment.
- Distribute modeling dough and transparent plastic strips.

Explore

- Verify that groups' cylinders are very close in diameter to their spheres.
- Have groups pair up to do the follow-up.

Summarize

- Ask groups what they discovered about the relationship of a sphere's volume to a cylinder's volume.
- Talk about how a sphere's volume can be found from the related cylinder.
- Ask students to estimate the amount of empty space in a tennis ball can. *(optional)*

Assignment Choices

Unassigned choices from earlier problems

Problem 5.1

- Using modeling dough, make a sphere with a diameter between 2 inches and 3.5 inches.

- Using a strip of transparent plastic, make a cylinder with an open top and bottom that fits snugly around your sphere. Trim the height of the cylinder to match the height of the sphere. Tape the cylinder together so that it remains rigid.

- Now, flatten the sphere so that it fits snugly in the bottom of the cylinder. Mark the height of the flattened sphere on the cylinder.

height of cylinder

height of empty space

height of flattened sphere

A. Measure and record the height of the cylinder, the height of the empty space, and the height of the flattened sphere.

B. What is the relationship between the volume of the sphere and the volume of the cylinder?

Remove the modeling dough from the cylinder, and save the cylinder for the next problem.

■ **Problem 5.1 Follow-Up**

Compare your results with the results of a group that made a larger or smaller sphere. Did the other group find the same relationship between the volume of the sphere and the volume of the cylinder?

Answers to Problem 5.1

A. Answers will vary.

B. The volume of the sphere is about two thirds the volume of the cylinder.

Answer to Problem 5.1 Follow-Up

The relationship between the volume of a sphere and the volume of a cylinder with the same radius and height is always the same: the sphere's volume is about two thirds the cylinder's volume.

Comparing Cones and Cylinders

In the last problem, you discovered the relationship between the volume of a sphere and the volume of a cylinder. In this problem, you will look for a relationship between the volume of a cone and the volume of a cylinder.

Problem 5.2

- Roll a piece of stiff paper into a cone shape so that the tip touches the bottom of your cylinder.

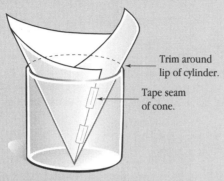

Trim around
lip of cylinder.

Tape seam
of cone.

- Tape the cone shape along the seam and trim it to form a cone with the same height as the cylinder.

- Fill the cone to the top with sand or rice, and empty the contents into the cylinder. Repeat this as many times as needed to completely fill the cylinder.

What is the relationship between the volume of the cone and the volume of the cylinder?

Answer to Problem 5.2

The volume of the cone is one third the volume of the cylinder.

Comparing Cones and Cylinders

At a Glance

Grouping: whole class or small groups

Launch

- Talk about the experiment.
- Conduct the experiment as a demonstration, or distribute sand or rice to each group.
- Have groups work on the problem and follow-up.

Explore

- Help any group that is having trouble making and trimming a cone the height of their cylinder.

Summarize

- Ask groups what they discovered about the relationship of a cone's volume to a cylinder's volume.
- Talk about how a cone's volume can be found from the related cylinder.
- Discuss ACE question 12 as a class. (*optional*)

Assignment Choices

ACE questions 1–4, 8, 12, and unassigned choices from earlier problems; Problem 5.3 could also be assigned as homework

Melting Ice Cream

At a Glance

Grouping: *individuals,*
then pairs

Launch

- Tell the story of the trip to the ice cream parlor.
- Conduct an experiment to demonstrate what happens in the problem. *(optional)*
- Have individuals work on the problem and follow-up and check answers in pairs.

Explore

- If students are having trouble, help them understand how their work in Problems 5.1 and 5.2 relates to this problem.

Summarize

- Ask students to share their answers and reasoning.
- Make sure two solution methods are shared: applying the relationships found in the previous work, and comparing the actual volumes of the shapes.
- Discuss the follow-up.

Assignment Choices

ACE questions 5–7, 9–11, and unassigned choices from earlier problems

Assessment

It is appropriate to use Check-Up 2 after this problem.

■ **Problem 5.2 Follow-Up**

If a cone, a cylinder, and a sphere have the same radius and the same height, what is the relationship between the volumes of the three shapes?

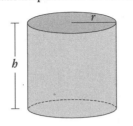 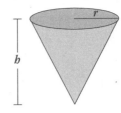 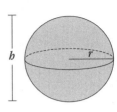

5.3 Melting Ice Cream

Olga and Serge buy ice cream from Chilly's Ice Cream Parlor. They think about buying an ice cream cone to bring back to Olga's little sister but decide the ice cream would melt before they got back home. Serge wonders, "If the ice cream all melts into the cone, will it fill the cone?"

Problem 5.3

Olga gets a scoop of ice cream in a cone, and Serge gets a scoop in a cylindrical cup. Each container has a height of 8 centimeters and a radius of 4 centimeters, and each scoop of ice cream is a sphere with a radius of 4 centimeters.

A. If Serge allows his ice cream to melt, will it fill his cup exactly? Explain.

B. If Olga allows her ice cream to melt, will it fill her cone exactly? Explain.

■ **Problem 5.3 Follow-Up**

How many scoops of ice cream of the size above can be packed into each container?

Answer to Problem 5.2 Follow-Up

See page 56e.

Answers to Problem 5.3

A. The cylindrical cup has a volume of $\pi \times 4^2 \times 8$ or about 402 cm^3. The spherical scoop of ice cream has two thirds the cylinder's volume, or about 268 cm^3. If the ice cream melts, it will not completely fill the cup.

B. The cone has the same height and radius as the cup, so its volume is one third the cup's volume, or about 134 cm^3. The ice cream has twice this volume, so if it melts it will overflow the cone.

Answer to Problem 5.3 Follow-Up

See page 56e.

Applications • Connections • Extensions

As you work on these ACE questions, use your calculator whenever you need it.

Applications

1. The city of La Agua has water storage tanks in three different shapes: a cylinder, a cone, and a sphere. Each tank has a radius of 20 ft and a height of 40 ft.

   a. Sketch each tank, and label its dimensions.

   b. What is the volume of the cylindrical tank?

   c. What is the volume of the conical tank?

   d. What is the volume of the spherical tank?

2. **a.** Find the volume of the cylinder, cone, and sphere shown below.

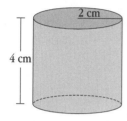
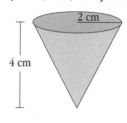
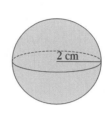

   b. How do the volumes of the three shapes compare?

3. An ice cream cone has a radius of 1 in and a height of 5 in. If a scoop of ice cream is a sphere with a radius of 1 in, how many scoops can be packed into the cone?

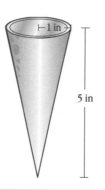

1a.

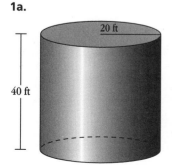

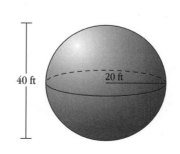

Answers

Applications

1a. See below left.

1b. about 50,265 ft³

1c. $\frac{1}{3} \times 50265 =$ about 16,755 ft³

1d. $\frac{2}{3} \times 50265 =$ about 33,510 ft³

2a. *cylinder:* about 50.3 cm³, *cone:* about 16.8 cm³, *sphere:* about 33.5 cm³

2b. Since all three shapes have the same height and radius, the cylinder's volume is three times the cone's volume, and the sphere's volume is twice the cone's volume. Or, the cone's volume is one third the cylinder's volume, and the sphere's volume is two thirds the cylinder's volume.

3. Using the relationship between this cone and a cylinder of height 5 in, the volume of the cone is $\frac{1}{3} \times \pi \times 1^2 \times 5 \approx 5.24$ in³. Using the relationship between this sphere and a cylinder of height 2 in, the volume of the scoop is $\frac{2}{3} \times \pi \times 1^2 \times 2 \approx 4.19$ in. It would take $5.24 \div 4.19 \approx 1.25$ scoops to fill the cone.

4. The cylindrical cup holds about 88.4 cm³ of frozen yogurt; the cone holds about 113 cm³. If the club wants to raise the most money possible, and they think an equal number of customers will buy the cup as the cone, the club should buy the cup.

5. The cone container is the best buy because it holds the most popcorn per dollar. *Cone:* volume ≈ 3142 cm³; popcorn is 3142 ÷ 2.50 ≈ 1257 cm³ per dollar. *Cylinder:* volume ≈ 4021 cm³; popcorn is 4021 ÷ 3.75 ≈ 1072 cm³ per dollar. *Box:* volume = 3600 cm³; popcorn is 3600 ÷ 3.50 ≈ 1029 cm³ per dollar. (Note: You may want to discuss with the class what is meant by "best buy." Some students may claim that the one that requires the least packaging material is the best buy. Also, this question asks about the best buy for the customer; ACE question 4 concerns the best deal for the seller.)

4. The track-and-field club is planning a frozen yogurt sale to raise money for new equipment. The club needs to buy containers to hold the yogurt. They must choose between the cup and cone shown below. The containers cost the same amount of money. The club plans to charge customers $1.25 for a serving of yogurt. Which container should the club buy? Why?

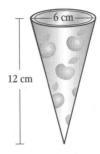

5. Fernando collected popcorn containers from several local movie theaters and recorded the prices and dimensions of the containers. Which is the best buy? Explain your answer.

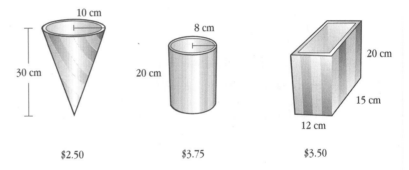

$2.50 $3.75 $3.50

Connections

6. A soft drink can is a cylinder with a radius of 3 cm and a height of 12 cm.

   a. Sketch a soft drink can, and label its dimensions.

   b. What is the circumference of the can?

   c. What is the volume of the can?

   d. What is the surface area of the can?

   e. How many cans of soda would it take to fill a liter bottle? (A liter bottle contains 1000 cm³.)

Extensions

7. Some Inuit Indians build igloos shaped like hemispheres (halves of a sphere). Some Hopi Indians in Arizona build adobes shaped like rectangular boxes. Suppose an igloo has an inner diameter of 40 ft.

   a. Describe the shape of a Hopi dwelling that would provide the same amount of living space as the igloo described above.

   b. For a Hopi dwelling to have the same amount of floor space as the igloo described above, what should the dimensions of the floor be?

Connections

6a.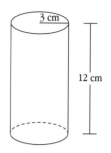

6b. $2\pi \times 3 \approx 18.8$ cm

6c. $9\pi \times 12 \approx 339$ cm³

6d. The ends each have an area of about 28.3 cm² and the lateral surface has an area of about 226 cm² for a total surface area of about 283 cm².

6e. It would take $\frac{1000}{339}$ = about 3 cans of soda to fill a liter bottle.

Extensions

7a. The igloo's volume is $\frac{1}{2} \times \frac{2}{3} \times \pi(20^2) \times 40 \approx$ 16,755 ft³. Possible answer: If the Hopi make an adobe with a 40-ft-square base, it would have to be 16,755 ÷ 1600 ≈ 10.5 ft high to have the same volume as the igloo.

7b. The igloo has $\pi(20^2) \approx$ 1257 ft² of floor space. The dimensions of the adobe's rectangular floor would have to be multiplied to give 1257; for example, 20 ft by about 63 ft. (Note: An infinite number of dimensions will work, including a square base of about 35.45 ft by 35.45 ft.)

8a. The submarine is constructed from a hemisphere, a cylinder, and a cone, so we must add the volumes of all three. *Hemisphere:* $\frac{1}{2} \times \frac{2}{3} \times \pi \times 3^2 \times 6 \approx 56.5$ in³; *cylinder:* $\pi \times 3^2 \times 12 \approx 339.3$ in³; *cone:* $\frac{1}{3} \times \pi \times 3^2 \times 4 \approx 37.7$ in³. The total volume is about 56.5 + 339.3 + 37.7 = 433.5 in³.

8b. about $433.5 \times 100^3 = 433,500,000$ ft³

9a. A sphere with radius 2.5 cm.

9b. A cylinder with radius 2.5 cm and height 5 cm.

9c. A cone with radius 2.5 cm and height 5 cm.

9d. The cylinder has the least amount of wasted space.

10. Possible answer: The cube has a volume of 1000 cm³. A cylinder with a radius of 5 cm has a base area of about 78.5 cm² and would need a height of $1000 \div 78.5 \approx 12.7$ cm. A cone with the same base would need three times the height, or about 38.1 cm, to have the same volume.

---

8. Laurie made a scale model of a submarine for her science class.

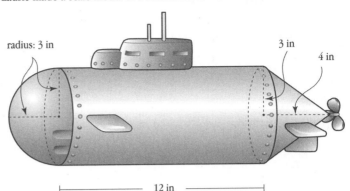

radius: 3 in   3 in   4 in

12 in

a. What is the volume of Laurie's model?

b. If 1 in on the model represents 100 ft on the actual submarine, what is the volume of the actual submarine?

9. a. Give the dimensions of the largest sphere that will fit inside a cubic box with 5-cm edges.

b. Give the dimensions of the largest cylinder that will fit inside a cubic box with 5-cm edges.

c. Give the dimensions of the largest cone that will fit inside a cubic box with 5-cm edges.

d. Which shape—sphere, cylinder, or cone—fits best inside the cubic box? That is, for which shape is there the least space between the shape and the box?

10. The edges of a cube measure 10 cm. Describe the dimensions of a cylinder and a cone with the same volume as the cube. (Hint: Starting with the cylinder is easier.) Explain your reasoning.

11. Pearl measures the circumference of a sphere and finds that it is 54 cm. What is the volume of the sphere? Explain.

12. The shapes below are pyramids. A pyramid is named for the shape of its base. The left shape is a triangular pyramid, the center shape is a square pyramid, and the right shape is a pentagonal pyramid. The sides of all pyramids are triangles.

    a. As the number of sides in the base of a pyramid increases, what happens to the shape of the pyramid?

    b. Describe a method for finding the surface area of a pyramid.

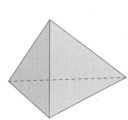 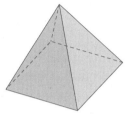 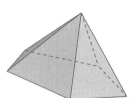

---

11. about 2664 cm³; Possible reasoning: Think of the sphere inside a cylinder. The circumference of the base of the cylinder would be 54 cm, giving a radius of $\frac{54}{2\pi} \approx 8.6$ cm. The height of the cylinder would be twice the radius, or 17.2 cm. The volume of the cylinder would be about 3996 cm³, so the volume of the sphere is about $\frac{2}{3} \times 3996 = 2664$ cm³.

12a. As the number of sides in the base increases, the pyramid looks more and more like a cone.

12b. The surface area can be found by adding the areas of the triangles (finding the area of one triangle and multiplying by the number of triangles) to the area of the base.

Possible Answers

Note: In reading students' answers, if you are unsure of how well they understand these ideas, you might give them the dimensions of some cones, cylinders, and spheres and ask them to find their volumes.

1. See page 56f.

2. You can think of a cylinder with the same radius as the sphere and a height of twice the radius. Since the sphere's volume will be two thirds the cylinder's volume, you can find the volume of the sphere by finding the volume of the cylinder first. Multiply the area of the base of the cylinder (πr^2) by its height ($2r$), and then multiply by $\frac{2}{3}$ to find the volume of the sphere.

3. You can think of a cylinder with the same radius and height as the cone. The cone will have one third the volume of the cylinder, so the volume of the cone is $\frac{1}{3}\pi r^2 h$. Or, as $h = 2r$, the volume of the cone is $\frac{2}{3}\pi r^3$.

In this investigation, you studied the relationships between the volumes of a cone, a sphere, and a cylinder with the same radius and height. These questions will help you summarize what you have learned:

1. If a cone, a cylinder, and a sphere have the same radius and height, describe the relationships among the volume of the cone, the volume of the sphere, and the volume of the cylinder. Use examples and sketches to illustrate your answer.

2. If you know the radius of a sphere, how can you find the sphere's volume?

3. If you know the radius and height of a cone, how can you find the cone's volume?

Think about your answers to these questions, discuss your ideas with other students and your teacher, and then write a summary of your findings in your journal.

Tips for the Linguistically Diverse Classroom

Original Rebus The Original Rebus technique is described in detail in *Getting to Know Connected Mathematics*. Students make a copy of the text before it is discussed. During the discussion, they generate their own rebuses for words they do not understand; the words are made comprehensible through pictures, objects, or demonstrations. Example: Question 2—Key phrases for which students might make rebuses are *radius of a sphere* (sphere with radius indicated), *sphere's volume* (shading added to the sphere rebus).

TEACHING THE INVESTIGATION

5.1 • Comparing Spheres and Cylinders

This problem is intended to help students develop a visual image of the relationship between the volume of a sphere and the volume of a cone. Often, formulas are given to students with little or no justification. This hands-on experiment will give students experiences in which they may discover for themselves the reasonableness of the formula for finding volume.

Launch

For the Teacher: Experiment or Demonstration

It's more effective if students have the opportunity to experiment on their own, but some teachers use Problems 5.1 and 5.2 as a demonstration to save time. If you choose to conduct the experiments as a class demonstration, try to create more than one example, and leave the containers on display so students can experiment with them later. You may want to purchase commercially available transparent containers (often sold in mathematics-supply catalogs and stores), which can be filled with colored water or sand and used to explore volume relationships.

As a demonstration, some teachers have had success using a tennis ball and creating a cylinder, with an open top and bottom, that matches the height and diameter of the tennis ball. Place the cylinder on a piece of paper, and put the ball into the cylinder. Pour sand into the cylinder, shaking it gently so that the sand settles in the empty space around the ball. Carefully lift the ball out of the cylinder, and measure the volume the sand occupies. It will be about one third the volume of the cylinder, which means the sphere occupied two thirds of the cylinder.

Hold up one of your sample cylinders.

How might you find the volume of this cylinder?

Hold up a sphere with a similar diameter.

How do you think the volumes of these two solids compare? Which has the greater volume?

After students make their guesses, talk to them about the experiment in Problem 5.1. Distribute modeling dough (vary the amount so the spheres students create will be of different sizes) and a strip of transparent plastic to each group of two or three students.

Explore

As groups work on the problem, make sure that they create spheres and that the cylinders they make are very close in diameter to their spheres.

If students follow the directions for the experiment carefully, they will find that the sphere's volume is about two thirds of the cylinder's volume. In other words, the flattened sphere will occupy about two thirds of the cylinder.

Have students do the follow-up when they and another group near them have finished working on the problem.

Summarize

Ask groups to share what they discovered about the relationship of a sphere's volume to a cylinder's volume. It should be clear from their measurements that the sphere's volume is about two thirds the cylinder's volume. The relationship can be left in this verbal form. Some students, however, may be able to write this relationship as a formula:

$$\text{Volume of the sphere} = \tfrac{2}{3}\pi r^2(h)$$

Some might be ready to understand that as the height of the sphere is twice its radius, $2r$ may be substituted for h:

$$\text{Volume of the sphere} = \tfrac{2}{3}\pi r^2(2r)$$

If some students focus on the relationship between the height of the empty space and the height of the sphere—saying that the height of the empty space is half the height of the flattened sphere—help refocus them on comparing the measures to the whole, the cylinder. The height of the flattened sphere is two thirds the height of the cylinder, and the height of the empty space is one third the height of the cylinder.

Help students form a visual image of the relationship between a cylinder's volume and a sphere's volume by using an illustration like the one below. To find the sphere's volume, students can visualize a cylinder with the same height and radius as the sphere, find the volume of the cylinder, and take two thirds of it.

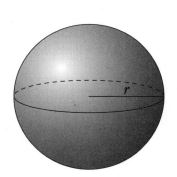

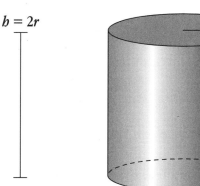

$h = 2r$

To find the volume
of a sphere,

start by thinking of a cylinder
with the same radius and height.

Students will probably see the formula for the volume of a sphere, $\frac{4}{3}\pi r^3$, in books, so it may be worth talking about how the $\frac{2}{3}$ they found becomes $\frac{4}{3}$:

$$\text{Volume of the sphere} = \frac{2}{3}\pi r^2(h)$$
$$= \frac{2}{3}\pi r^2(2r)$$
$$= \frac{4}{3}\pi r^3$$

Offer another example to assess their understanding.

What is the volume of a sphere that has a radius of 5 centimeters?

As an extension activity for students who seem to have a good grasp of the relationship between the volumes of spheres and cylinders, have students estimate the amount of empty space in a cylindrical tennis ball container with three tennis balls inside. The height of the container is equal to three times the diameter of a tennis ball, and the diameter of the container equals that of a tennis ball. Thus, the volume of the container is $3(2r)(\pi r^2) = 6\pi r^3$. The volume of a tennis ball is $\frac{4}{3}\pi r^3$, so three tennis balls have a volume of $3(\frac{4}{3}\pi r^3) = 4\pi r^3$. This means that the empty space is $2\pi r^3$. (Don't push for this much symbolic representation if you have students do this problem. Their work will likely be a series of multiplication problems, which is fine at this stage.)

Students will need their cylinders for the next problem. You may also want them to re-form and save their dough spheres for Problem 7.1, when they can use the water-displacement method to directly measure the volumes of their spheres.

5.2 • Comparing Cones and Cylinders

In this problem, students conduct an experiment to explore the relationship between the volume of a cone and the volume of a cylinder. They construct a cone with the same radius and height as the cylinder they made in Problem 5.1. The student edition and Transparency 5.2 illustrate the process. Then, they use the cone to fill the cylinder with sand or rice.

To save time, this could be conducted as a demonstration, but students will develop a greater understanding of cones if they make one and do the filling themselves.

Launch

Talk about the experiment in Problem 5.2, and distribute sand or rice to each group. Have students work in their groups to construct a cone and then compare the volumes of the cone and the cylinder. When groups are finished, have them move on to the follow-up.

Explore

As groups explore the problem, help those who are having trouble making a cone or trimming it down to the height of their cylinder.

Summarize

Ask groups to share what they learned about the relationship of a cone's volume to a cylinder's volume. It takes three cones full of sand or rice to fill the cylinder. Students should be able to explain this discovery in words: for a cone and a cylinder of the same height and radius, the volume of the cone is one third the volume of the cylinder.

Some students may be able to write this relationship as a formula:

$$\text{Volume of a cone} = \tfrac{1}{3}\pi r^2 h$$

Clear plastic containers are great for demonstrating this relationship and will help students develop a visual image of it. You can also help students to see this relationship by using an illustration like the one below.

$h = 2r$

To find the volume
of a cone,

start by thinking of a cylinder
with the same radius and height
(in this case, twice the radius).

Offer another example to assess their understanding.

> What is the volume of a cone with a radius of 5 centimeters and a height of 10 centimeters?

ACE question 12, which asks students to think about pyramids, makes a nice extension for the summary. As the number of sides in the base of a pyramid increases, the shape of the pyramid approaches that of a cone. The volume of a pyramid is found the same way the volume of a cone is found.

If your students have made sense of Problem 5.2, it would be appropriate to assign Problem 5.3 as homework rather than exploring it in class. Students could solve the problem at home, and the class could summarize it the next day.

• **Melting Ice Cream**

In this problem, students use their new knowledge about volume to explore whether the volume of a sphere will fill a cone or a cylinder with the same dimensions. This is a short problem and could be assigned as homework after Problem 5.2.

Launch

If you decide to do this problem in class, tell the story of Olga and Serge's trip to the ice cream parlor. Make sure students understand that the ice cream melts into the containers. While the problem is designed to have students use what they already know to make comparisons, a demonstration may still be useful—if you don't mind ice cream melting in your classroom! Such an experiment would also raise the issue of whether the volume of the ice cream will remain the same as it melts. The science teacher may be able to help coordinate an experiment to enhance students' mathematics work.

Have students work on the problem and the follow-up individually and check answers in pairs.

Explore

For students who are struggling, ask how this problem is similar to Problems 5.1 and 5.2 and how it is different from them. Guide a discussion that helps them see how to apply what they have learned about volume to this problem.

Summarize

Have students share their conclusions and reasoning. Some will reason from the relationships they found in Problems 5.1 and 5.2; some may calculate the volumes of all three shapes and compare them. Be sure both ideas are presented. From their explanations, you will be able to assess their understanding of the volumes of cones, spheres, and cylinders.

Discuss students' solutions to the follow-up. Most will understand that the cone only holds half of a scoop. It may take more discussion to help all students understand that the cylinder holds one and a half scoops.

Additional Answers

Answer to Problem 5.2 Follow-Up

The cone's volume is one third the cylinder's volume, and the sphere's volume is two thirds the cylinder's volume. Therefore, the cone's volume is half that of the sphere's volume. Some students may notice that the volumes of the sphere and cone together will exactly fill the cylinder. Some may be able to write the relationships as formulas: volume of cylinder = $\pi r^2 h$; volume of sphere = $\frac{2}{3}\pi r^2 h = \frac{2}{3}\pi r^2(2r) = \frac{4}{3}\pi r^3$; volume of cone = $\frac{1}{3}\pi r^2 h = \frac{1}{3}\pi r^2(2r) = \frac{2}{3}\pi r^3$.

Answer to Problem 5.3 Follow-Up

The cup will hold about 402 cm³ of ice cream; the cone will hold about 134 cm³ of ice cream. Since one scoop of ice cream has a volume of about 268 cm³, half a scoop will pack into the cone, and one and a half scoops will pack into the cup.

Mathematical Reflections

1. If a cone, a cylinder, and a sphere all have the same radius and height, the volume of the cone is one third the volume of the cylinder. The volume of the sphere is two thirds the volume of the cylinder. The volume of the cone is one half the volume of the sphere. For example, suppose they all have a height of 10 cm and a radius of 5 cm:

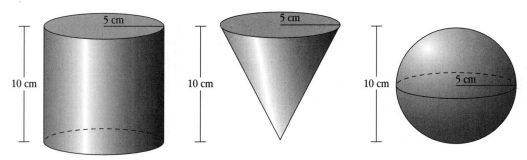

The cylinder's volume is $25\pi \times 10$ = about 785 cm². The cone's volume is one third of 785 cm², or about 262 cm². The sphere's volume is two thirds of 785 cm², or about 523 cm².

Scaling Boxes

In this investigation, students study the effects of changing the dimensions or the volume of a rectangular prism in the context of designing compost containers. Students explore two central ideas: How do you build a rectangular container with twice the volume of a given container? What effect does doubling each dimension of a rectangular container have on the volume and surface area?

Problem 6.1, Building a Bigger Box, asks students to explore what happens to the volume of a box if each of its dimensions are doubled. Problem 6.2, Scaling Up the Compost Box, challenges students to design a box with a given volume. Problem 6.3, Looking at Similar Prisms, brings in the ideas studied in the *Stretching and Shrinking* unit. Students are asked to apply their knowledge of similarity and scale factors to three-dimensional rectangular boxes.

Mathematical and Problem-Solving Goals

■ *To apply strategies for finding the volumes of rectangular prisms to designing boxes with given specifications*

■ *To investigate the effects of varying the dimensions of rectangular prisms on volume and surface area and vice versa*

Materials		
Problem	**For students**	**For the teacher**
All	Graphing calculators	Transparencies 6.1 to 6.3 (optional), demonstration compost boxes (real compost boxes or scale models; optional)
6.1	Centimeter cubes (optional), centimeter grid paper (provided as a blackline master), scissors, transparent tape	
6.2	Centimeter cubes (optional), centimeter grid paper, scissors, transparent tape	

Scaling Boxes

Discarded paper, plastic, and glass is not the only urban-waste disposal problem. Decaying organic waste from food, grass, and leaves gives off unpleasant odors and explosive methane gas.

© 1991 by Sidney Harris. From *You Want Proof? I'll Give You Proof!* W. H. Freeman, New York.

Composting is a method for turning organic waste into rich soil. Composting has been used for thousands of years on farms and in gardens. Today, many people have indoor compost boxes that break down kitchen waste quickly and with little odor. The secret is in the worms!

Building a Bigger Box

Launch

- Read the news article to the class, and discuss the introduction and Deshondra's project.
- Have each student make a model of each box, confer with a partner, and answer the follow-up questions.

Explore

- Check that students double each dimension to make the 2-4-6 box.
- Suggest that students organize their findings in a table.

Summarize

- Discuss the increase in surface area and volume that results from doubling the side lengths.
- Ask if it matters which side of a compost box is open.
- Talk about the ratios in the follow-up questions.

Assignment Choices

ACE questions 6, 9, 10, and unassigned choices from earlier problems (you may want to supply isometric dot paper for 6)

Recipe for a 1-2-3 Compost Box
- Start with an open rectangular wood box that is 1 foot high, 2 feet wide, and 3 feet long. We call this a *1-2-3 box*.
- Mix 10 pounds of shredded newspaper with 15 quarts of water, and put the mixture in the 1-2-3 box.
- Add a few handfuls of soil.
- Add about 1000 redworms (about 1 pound).

Every day, mix collected kitchen waste with the soil in the box. The worms will do the rest of the work, turning the waste into new soil. A 1-2-3 box will decompose about 0.5 pound of garbage each day.

Source: Woldumar Nature Center, Lansing, Michigan.

6.1 Building a Bigger Box

Deshondra chose composting as the topic of her science project. She plans to build a compost box at home and to keep records of the amount of soil produced over several weeks.

Problem 6.1

Deshondra wants her compost box to be larger than the 1-2-3 box. She decides to double each edge of the 1-2-3 box.

A. Use grid paper to make scale models of a 1-2-3 box and Deshondra's 2-4-6 box. The boxes should have open tops.

B. Deshondra wants to increase the composting capacity of her box by the same factor as the volume. How much shredded paper and water will she need for her 2-4-6 compost box?

C. How many worms will she need?

D. How much plywood will she need to build the box?

E. How many pounds of garbage will the box be able to decompose in one day?

Save your model of the 1-2-3 box for the next problem.

Answers to Problem 6.1

A. See page 67f.

B. She will need 80 pounds of shredded paper and 120 quarts of water.

C. She will need 8000 worms (8 pounds).

D. She will need 2(8) + 2(12) + 24 = 64 ft² of plywood (there is no lid).

E. The 2-4-6 box has a volume of 48 ft³, which is $\frac{48}{6}$ = 8 times the volume of the 1-2-3 box. Thus, the 2-4-6 box can decompose 8×0.5 = 4 pounds of garbage a day.

■ Problem 6.1 Follow-Up

1. Find the ratio of the length of each side of the 1-2-3 box to the length of the corresponding side of the 2-4-6 box.

2. Find the ratio of the surface area of the 1-2-3 box to the surface area of the 2-4-6 box.

3. Find the ratio of the volume of the 1-2-3 box to the volume of the 2-4-6 box.

 6.2 ## Scaling Up the Compost Box

Ms. Fernandez's class decides that building and maintaining a compost box would be a fascinating project. One student suggests that they could earn money for a class trip by selling the worms and soil they produce to a local nursery.

The class estimates that they throw away about 1 pound of organic waste each day, rather than the 0.5 pound specified in the 1-2-3 box recipe. They need to adjust the recipe to build a box large enough to decompose all the garbage they will produce.

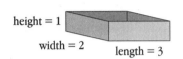

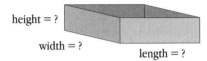

> ### Problem 6.2
>
> How could Ms. Fernandez's class scale up the recipe for the 1-2-3 box to make a box that will decompose 1 pound of organic waste each day?
>
> **A.** What box dimensions would give the required space for the new quantity of organic waste?
>
> **B.** Use grid paper to make a scale model of a box that would decompose 1 pound of garbage per day. The box should have an open top.

■ Problem 6.2 Follow-Up

1. How much plywood will the class need to construct their box?

2. How much shredded paper and water will they need?

3. How many worms will they need?

Answers to Problem 6.1 Follow-Up

See page 67f.

Answers to Problem 6.2

A. The 1-2-3 box has a volume of 6 ft³. It can accommodate 0.5 pound of waste, so the new box would need twice the volume, or 12 ft³, to handle 1 pound of waste. A few possibilities are a 3-4-1 box, a 1-1-12 box, a 2-2-3 box, and a 2-6-1 box.

B. Scale models will vary.

Answers to Problem 6.2 Follow-Up

See page 67g.

At a Glance

Grouping: individuals

Launch

■ Talk with the class about how to design a compost box based on how much garbage it will decompose.

■ Have each student make a model of the new box, confer with a partner, and answer the follow-up questions.

Explore

■ Circulate as students work.

■ Allow students to discover and correct their own mistakes.

Summarize

■ Have students share the boxes they made, giving the dimensions and stating the volume.

■ Help the class compare the various boxes.

■ Talk about the follow-up questions.

Assignment Choices

ACE questions 1, 3–5, 7, 11, and unassigned choices from earlier problems (you may want to supply isometric dot paper for 4 and 5)

Looking at Similar Prisms

At a Glance

***Grouping:
small groups***

Launch

- Ask about the volume and surface area of a 1-2-3 box if its dimensions are tripled or quadrupled.

- Review the information in the student edition about similar figures and scale factors.

- Have groups explore the problem and follow-up.

Explore

- Have groups design boxes similar to a 1-2-3 box and work together to find their volumes and surface areas.

Summarize

- Help the class summarize their discoveries.

- Assess how well students understand scale factor and similarity in the context of three-dimensional shapes.

- Discuss ACE questions 19–22 in class. *(optional)*

6.3 Looking at Similar Prisms

In *Stretching and Shrinking*, you studied similar two-dimensional figures. The ideas you learned in that unit also apply to three-dimensional figures. For example, two rectangular prisms are similar if the ratios of the lengths of corresponding edges are equal.

The *scale factor* is the number that each dimension of one rectangular prism must be multiplied by to get the dimensions of a similar prism. For example, a 1-2-3 box is similar to a 2-4-6 box. The scale factor from the small box to the large box is 2, because the edge lengths of the small box must be multiplied by 2 to get the corresponding edge lengths of the large box.

Problem 6.3

A. Find three other rectangular boxes that are similar to a 1-2-3 box, and give their dimensions. Give the scale factor from a 1-2-3 box to each box you find.

B. **1.** Calculate the surface area of each box you found in part A, and tell how the result compares to the surface area of a 1-2-3 box.

  2. How is the change in surface area from a 1-2-3 box to a similar box related to the scale factor from the 1-2-3 box to the similar box?

C. **1.** Calculate the volume of each box you found in part A, and tell how the result compares to the volume of a 1-2-3 box.

  2. How is the change in volume from a 1-2-3 box to a similar box related to the scale factor from the 1-2-3 box to the similar box?

■ **Problem 6.3 Follow-Up**

Are all rectangular prisms similar? Explain your answer.

Assignment Choices

ACE questions 2, 8, 12–22, and unassigned choices from earlier problems

Assessment

It is appropriate to use the quiz after this problem.

Answers to Problem 6.3

A. Possible answer: A 1.5-3-4.5 box, a 3-6-9 box, and a 4-8-12 box, with scale factors of 1.5, 3, and 4, respectively.

B. 1. Possible answer: 1.5-3-4.5 box, 36 ft²; 3-6-9 box, 144 ft²; 4-8-12 box, 256 ft²; As a 1-2-3 box has a surface area of 16 ft², these boxes have, respectively, 2.25 times, 9 times, and 16 times as much surface area.

  2. The surface area grows by the square of the scale factor.

C. See page 67g.

Answer to Problem 6.3 Follow-Up

Not all rectangular prisms are similar. For example, a 1-2-3 box is not similar to a 1-4-3 box because the ratios of corresponding edges are not equal.

Applications • Connections • Extensions

As you work on these ACE questions, use your calculator whenever you need it. Remember that height is the first number when dimensions of a box are given.

Applications

1. **a.** What is the volume of a 1-2-2 box?

    b. What is the surface area of a closed 1-2-2 box?

2. **a.** What is the volume of a 1.5-1.5-3 box?

    b. What is the surface area of a closed 1.5-1.5-3 box?

3. **a.** What is the volume of a 2-4-1 box?

    b. What is the surface area of a closed 2-4-1 box?

4. **a.** Make a sketch of an open 2-2-3 box and an open 2-2-6 box. Label the edges of the boxes.

    b. Find the volume of each box in part a.

    c. Find the surface area of each box in part a.

    d. If you wanted to adapt the 1-2-3 compost box recipe for the boxes in part a, how many worms and how much paper and water would you need for each box?

5. **a.** Make a sketch of a 1-3-5 box. Label the edges of the box.

    b. Sketch three boxes that have twice the volume of a 1-3-5 box. Label each box with its dimensions.

Answers

Applications

1a. 4 ft^3

1b. 16 ft^2

2a. 6.75 ft^3

2b. 22.5 ft^2

3a. 8 ft^3

3b. 28 ft^2

4a. See below left.

4b. *2-2-3 box:* 12 ft^3, *2-2-6 box:* 24 ft^3

4c. *2-2-3 box:* 26 ft^2; *2-2-6 box:* 44 ft^2

4d. *2-2-3 box:* 2000 worms, 20 pounds of paper, and 30 quarts of water; *2-2-6 box:* 4000 worms, 40 pounds of paper, and 60 quarts of water

5a.
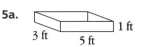
3 ft 5 ft 1 ft

5b. See below left.

4a.

2 ft 2 ft 3 ft 2 ft

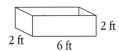
2 ft 2 ft 6 ft 2 ft

5b.

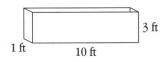
1 ft 10 ft 3 ft

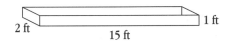
2 ft 15 ft 1 ft

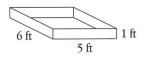
6 ft 5 ft 1 ft

6a. See below right.

6b. *1-ft cube: 1 ft³, 2-ft cube: 8 ft³, 3-ft cube: 27 ft³*

6c. *1-ft cube: 6 ft², 2-ft cube: 24 ft², 3-ft cube: 54 ft²*

6d. When the dimensions are doubled, the new volume is 8 times the original. When they are tripled, the new volume is 27 times the original. When they are quadrupled, the new volume is 64 times the original. In general, when the dimensions are increased n times, the new volume is n^3 times the original.

6e. When the dimensions are doubled, the new surface area is 4 times the original. When they are tripled, the new surface area is 9 times the original. When they are quadrupled, the new surface area is 16 times the original. In general, when the dimensions are increased n times, the new surface area is n^2 times the original.

7. If the Sunday papers were made from recycled paper, $\frac{500,000}{17} \approx 29,412$ tons of recycled paper would be required, and $29,412 \times 3.3 \approx 97,060$ yd³ of landfill would be saved. (Note: If you have information about the amount of paper recycled in your community, this might make a good discussion. Students could keep track of the paper thrown out—or saved for recycling—in their house in one week.)

8a. In a year, a family of four would produce $2.7 \times 4 \times 365 = 3942$ pounds of garbage and use $3942 \div 50 = 78.84$ ft³ of landfill.

---

6. **a.** Make scale drawings of three cubes: one with edges measuring 1 ft, one with edges measuring 2 ft, and one with edges measuring 3 ft. For each cube, tell what length in the drawing represents 1 ft. In other words, give the scale for each drawing.

b. Find the volume of each cube in part a.

c. Find the surface area of each cube in part a.

d. Describe what happens to the volume of a cube when the edge lengths are doubled, tripled, quadrupled, and so on.

e. Describe what happens to the surface area of a cube when the edge lengths are doubled, tripled, quadrupled, and so on.

7. For every ton of paper that is recycled, about 17 trees and 3.3 yd³ of landfill space are saved. In the United States, 500,000 trees are used each week to produce the Sunday papers. If one Sunday, all the newspapers were made from 100% recycled paper, how much landfill would be saved?

8. In the United States, an average of 2.7 pounds of garbage per person is delivered to available landfills each day. A cubic foot of compressed garbage weighs about 50 pounds.

a. Estimate the amount of landfill used by a family of four in one year.

b. Estimate the amount of landfill used by the families of all your classmates in one year. Assume each family has four people.

9. Each year the United States generates about 450 million cubic yards of solid waste. Mr. Costello's classroom is 42 ft long, 30 ft wide, and 12 ft high. How many rooms of this size would be needed to hold all this garbage?

6a. Scales will vary; the scale used below is 4 mm = 1 ft.

  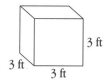

8b. Answers will vary. Over a year, the families of a class of 30 students would produce $30 \times 3942 = 118,260$ pounds of garbage and use $118,260 \div 50 \approx 2365$ ft³ of landfill.

9. The classroom will hold $42 \times 30 \times 12 = 15,120$ ft³ of garbage or $15,120 \div 3^3 = 560$ yd³. It would take $450,000,000 \div 560 \approx 803,571$ rooms of this size to hold the garbage.

Connections

10. Mary's class decides to build a cylindrical compost box. Mary calculates that a cylindrical container with a height of 2 ft and a radius of 1 ft would decompose 0.5 pound of garbage each day. She calls this container a *1-2 cylinder.*

1 ft
2 ft

    a. How does the volume of the 1-2 cylinder compare to the volume of the 1-2-3 box?

    b. How does the surface area of the 1-2 cylinder compare to the surface area of the 1-2-3 box?

    c. Mary's class estimates that they throw away about 1 pound of organic waste at school each day. What size cylinder should they build to handle this much waste?

11. At the movie theater, Ted is trying to decide whether to buy a large popcorn or two small popcorns. Both sizes come in cylindrical containers. Ted thinks that the heights of the containers are about the same and that the radius of the large container is about twice the radius of the small container. A large popcorn costs $3.00, and a small popcorn costs $1.50. To get the most popcorn for his $3.00, should Ted buy one large popcorn or two small popcorns? Explain your answer.

or ?

Connections

10. Note: This problem would make a good class discussion.

10a. The volume of a 1-2-3 box is 6 ft³. The volume of a 1-2 cylinder is about 6.28 ft³. The cylinder's volume is a little more than the box's volume.

10b. The surface area of a 1-2-3 box is 16 ft². The surface area of a 1-2 cylinder is about 15.7 ft². The cylinder requires a little less material than the box.

10c. See below left.

11. The larger container is the better buy; for twice the money, the larger size contains four times the popcorn because doubling the radius of a cylinder quadruples its volume. So, for $3.00 Ted can buy twice as much by buying one large popcorn.

10c. Mary's class needs a cylinder with twice the volume of a 1-2 cylinder. There are infinite sets of dimensions that would work; two are a 1-4 cylinder and a 1.41-2 cylinder. (Note: Students should see the similarity between how the volume and surface area of a cylinder grow if its dimensions are doubled and the doubling of the dimensions of a rectangular box. Help them see the limitations of doubling one dimension as a technique for doubling the volume. For a rectangular box, if one dimension is doubled, the volume is doubled. For a cylinder, if the height is doubled, the volume is doubled; but if the radius is doubled, the volume is quadrupled because the radius is squared when finding the volume. You could ask students: *Suppose Mary's class decides to double each dimension of the 1-2 cylinder. How will the new volume and surface area compare to the 1-2 cylinder?* The volume of a 2-4 cylinder is 8 times the volume of a 1-2 container. The surface area of a 2-4 cylinder is 4 times the surface area of a 1-2 cylinder.)

12a. 100 boxes

12b. 10 layers

12c. A total of 100 × 10 = 1000 boxes could be stored in the warehouse.

13. volume = 45 cubic units; surface area = 78 square units

14. volume = 2 cubic units; surface area = 10 square units

15. volume = 9 cubic units; surface area = 30 square units

12. The Whole Earth Compost Company builds and sells 1-2-3 compost boxes. They need to store a supply of the boxes in their warehouse to fill customers' orders. The sketch below shows a 1-2-3 box and the space in the warehouse allotted for the boxes.

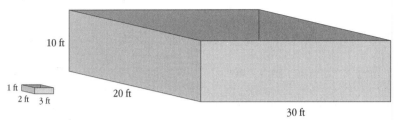

a. How many 1-2-3 boxes could be stored in one layer on the floor of the storage space?

b. How many layers of boxes could be stacked in the storage space?

c. How many boxes could be stored in the storage space?

In 13–15, find the volume and surface area of the box.

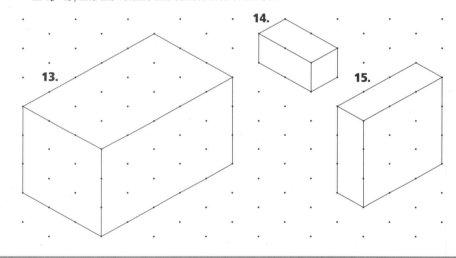

Extensions

16. Is the price of cereal directly related to the volume of the box? Collect some data to help you answer this question.

    a. Record the dimensions and prices of two or three different size boxes of the same cereal brand.

    b. Calculate the volume of each box.

    c. Calculate the cost per unit of volume for each box. Compare the results for the different boxes.

    d. Write a short report summarizing what you learned about the relationship between box size and cereal price.

17. The following sketch shows a "tilted box" in which the base, top, and smaller sides are rectangles, and the other two faces are non-rectangular parallelograms.

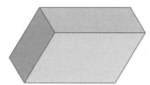

    a. What measurements would you need to find the volume of this box? How would you use these measurements to calculate the volume?

    b. What measurements would you need to find the surface area of this box? How would you use these measurements to calculate the surface area?

18. Think about a "sliceable" rectangular prism, such as a cake, a loaf of bread, or a brick of cheese.

    a. How many different ways can you slice such a prism into two pieces of equal volume?

    b. If the prism were a cube, how many ways could you slice it into two pieces of equal volume?

Extensions

16. Answers will vary. Students will probably discover that larger boxes tend to be better buys because the cost per unit volume is less. (Note: This ACE question makes a good project. Students will spend time collecting and analyzing real data and writing a report.)

17a. (Note: This situation is analogous to finding the area and perimeter of a parallelogram.) The length, width, and height of the tilted box will be needed to find its volume. The three measures would be multiplied together to find the volume.

17b. The surface area of each face would be calculated from the appropriate measures and added together to produce the total surface area.

18a. A prism can be sliced in an infinite number of ways to produce two pieces of equal volume.

18b. A cube can be sliced in an infinite number of ways to produce two pieces of equal volume.

19a. 2 to 1 or $\frac{2}{1}$

19b. 2 to 1 or $\frac{2}{1}$

19c. 4 to 1 or $\frac{4}{1}$

19d. 8 to 1 or $\frac{8}{1}$

20a. 3 to 1 or $\frac{3}{1}$

20b. 3 to 1 or $\frac{3}{1}$

20c. 9 to 1 or $\frac{9}{1}$

20d. 27 to 1 or $\frac{27}{1}$

21a. 4 to 1 or $\frac{4}{1}$

21b. 4 to 1 or $\frac{4}{1}$

21c. 16 to 1 or $\frac{16}{1}$

21d. 64 to 1 or $\frac{64}{1}$

22a. $25 \times 200 = 5000$ cm or 50 m

22b. $600 \times 200^3 =$ 4,800,000,000 cm^3 or 4800 m^3

22c. $250 \div 200^2 =$ 0.00625 m^2 or 62.5 cm^2

22d. **i.** height = $4 \times 200 = 800$ cm or 8 m, radius = $1.5 \times 200 = 300$ cm or 3 m
ii. about 226 m^3
iii. about 151 m^2 (Note: The top and bottom of the smokestack are open.)

---

19. The dimensions of cylinder A are twice the dimensions of cylinder B.

  a. What is the ratio of the radius of cylinder A to the radius of cylinder B?

  b. What is the ratio of the height of cylinder A to the height of cylinder B?

  c. What is the ratio of the surface area of cylinder A to the surface area of cylinder B?

  d. What is the ratio of the volume of cylinder A to the volume of cylinder B?

20. The dimensions of cylinder A are three times the dimensions of cylinder B. Repeat parts a–d of question 19 for these cylinders.

21. The dimensions of cylinder A are four times the dimensions of cylinder B. Repeat parts a–d of question 19 for these cylinders.

22. Natasha built a model cruise ship from a kit. She was trying to imagine what the actual cruise ship would look like. The scale factor from the model ship to the actual ship is 200.

  a. If the length of the model ship is 25 cm, what is the length of the actual ship?

  b. If the cold-storage space of the model has a capacity of 600 cm^3, what is the capacity of the cold-storage space of the actual ship?

  c. The area of the dance floor on the actual cruise ship is 250 m^2. What is the area of the dance floor on the model?

  d. The cylindrical smokestack on the model has a height of 4 cm and a radius of 1.5 cm.

   i. What are the dimensions of the smokestack on the actual ship?

   ii. What is the volume of the smokestack on the actual ship?

   iii. What is the surface area of the smokestack on the actual ship?

Mathematical Reflections

In this investigation, you learned how changing the dimensions of a rectangular box affects its volume and how changing the volume of a rectangular box affects its dimensions. These questions will help you summarize what you have learned:

1 Suppose you wanted to build a rectangular box with twice the volume of a given rectangular box. How could you determine the possible dimensions for the new box?

2 Describe how the volume and surface area of a rectangular prism change as each of its dimensions is doubled, tripled, quadrupled, and so on.

Think about your answers to these questions, discuss your ideas with other students and your teacher, and then write a summary of your findings in your journal.

Possible Answers

1. To double the volume, you could double one of the box's dimensions. Or, you could find three other dimensions that multiply together to give twice the volume of the original box.

2. If the dimensions of a rectangular prism are doubled, the new surface area is 4 times the original and the new volume is 8 times the original. If the dimensions are tripled, the new surface area is 9 times the original and the new volume is 27 times the original. If the dimensions are quadrupled, the new surface area is 16 times the original and the new volume is 64 times the original. In general, if the dimensions are increased by n, the new surface area is n^2 times the original and the new volume is n^3 times the original.

TEACHING THE INVESTIGATION

6.1 • Building a Bigger Box

In this problem, students investigate the effect that doubling the dimensions of a compost box has on its volume and surface area.

The recipe for the 1-2-3 compost box is taken from the experience of a group of young campers at the Woldumar Nature Center in Lansing, Michigan. During summer day camp, the campers composted their lunch remains each day in a compost box. It is fairly easy to do.

Launch

To introduce the topic, read the following article to the class.

State worms to receive leftovers

Some Massachusetts state employees soon will have some slimy colleagues who work for table scraps.

The Conservation Law Foundation, an environmental group, is donating about a kilogram of red worms that will be relegated to office-building basements. Their mission will be to eat leftover food that usually is thrown away. It's a dirty job but the worms don't mind doing it.

Three green plastic bins went to the Executive Office of Environmental Affairs. Inside each were some shredded newspapers and 600 to 5,000 worms, depending on their age and size.

"It does work and it saves us money," said Doug Foy, foundation executive director.

Reprinted with permission from Associated Press.

With the class, read the introduction to Problem 6.1 and the story of Deshondra's compost box. You might ask students to express their initial reactions to the questions.

> How will the scale factor of 2 affect the volume?

Distribute grid paper, scissors, and tape. Have each student make models of a 1-2-3 and a 2-4-6 box, check their efforts with a partner, and answer the follow-up questions.

Explore

To make their models, students can either cut flat patterns from grid paper, or they can cut out rectangles and tape them together.

As students work on their models, check that they double each dimension to make the 2-4-6 box. Remind students that there is more to the problem than just constructing the models: their models should help them answer parts B through E.

When students move on to the follow-up, suggest that they make a table to record the data from their two boxes. This will make finding the ratios easier. Their tables might have the following column heads:

Length (feet)	Width (feet)	Height (feet)	Volume (cubic feet)	Surface area (square feet)

Summarize

Hold up models of the two different box sizes. The fact that the volume goes from 6 cubic feet to 48 cubic feet (a factor of 2^3) while the dimensions only double usually amazes students.

The side lengths of the large box are twice the side lengths of the small box. Yet, how many small boxes will fit into a large box? *(8)* Can someone prove that? *(They can demonstrate this by combining their small models.)*

Why does it make sense that doubling all the length measurements increases the volume eight times?

Did doubling all the measures increase the surface area eight times? *(no)* How many times greater is the surface area of the large box than the surface area of the small box? *(4)*

Why does it make sense that doubling all the length measures made the surface area four times as great?

Ask whether it makes a difference which side of a compost box is left open. (A larger opening at the top provides better ventilation—worms, like people, need oxygen. If there is adequate ventilation, the worms will survive better, and hence more garbage will get processed. Also, the box will not be prone to the foul odors caused by anaerobic bacteria—the very stinky bacteria, often present in rotting garbage, that live only where there is a lack of oxygen.)

Talk about the ratios in the follow-up questions.

Do you see a pattern in the three ratios you found?

The ratio of the lengths of the sides is $\frac{1}{2}$. The ratio of the surface areas is $\frac{1}{4}$ or $\frac{1}{2^2}$. The ratio of the volumes is $\frac{1}{8}$ or $\frac{1}{2^3}$.

Tell students to save their models of the 1-2-3 boxes for the next problem.

• **Scaling Up the Compost Box**

In this problem, students design a box that will decompose 1 pound of garbage a day. This requires a box with twice the volume of a 1-2-3 box.

Launch

For the Teacher: A Worm Testimonial

A teacher from Oregon wrote the following: "Ever since I heard about worm boxes, I had planned on starting one. This activity offered a great excuse. I had a book on composting that suggested a ratio of 2.5 pounds of paper per cubic foot of space and 3 pounds of water for every pound of paper. My box was 20 in by 24 in by 12 in, so I started doing my math to figure out what I had to do to set this thing up. What a great activity for the kids. I went into class with a scale, newspaper, soil, two gallons of water, a mixing bin, some garbage from my kitchen and, of course, the worm box and worms. I was wearing a pin that said *Worms eat my garbage.* Kids noticed. They were excited. My pet worms are now happily digesting garbage under my table at school."

The class used the ratios the teacher supplied them to determine the amount of paper and other ingredients to put into the box. For home-work, they worked on Problem 6.2. If you decide to make a class worm box, you might propose the project after the class has had a chance to discuss Problem 6.2.

Talk with students about the idea of designing a compost box based on how much garbage it will decompose. Remind students that the compost boxes are open on top.

What is the surface area of a 1-2-3 box? *(16 square feet)* What is the volume of a 1-2-3 box? *(6 cubic feet)*

What feature of the box does the amount of garbage that is decom-posed each day relate to? *(the volume)*

If we double the amount of garbage, what feature of the 1-2-3 box will we need to double? *(the volume)*

Distribute grid paper, scissors, and tape. Have each student make a model of the new box to go along with their 1-2-3 box from Problem 6.1. Students should check their efforts with a partner, then answer the follow-up questions.

Explore

Circulate as students work. Some students will be tempted to just double the dimensions of the 1-2-3 box to create the new box, not thinking about what they did in Problem 6.1. Let them proceed; they will learn from their mistakes. Some students may make three or four new boxes before they get one that works.

Summarize

Have students share the boxes they made, giving their dimensions. You may want to record this information on the board for reference later in the summary. Ask students to report the volume for each size box. There are an infinite number of boxes with the necessary volume. Most students will make one of these three: a 2-2-3 box, a 1-4-3 box, or a 1-2-6 box.

If some students doubled each dimension, their box will have a volume eight times that of the 1-2-3 box. Point out that their box obviously has a greater volume than the problem requires, and ask them to explain why this is so.

Help students compare the various boxes.

> Of the boxes made by the people in our class, which will require the least material to make? Which will require the most material?

> Which model would be the most practical if we wanted to make a real box for our classroom?

Discuss the remaining follow-up questions.

6.3 • Looking at Similar Prisms

In this problem, students generalize the findings from Problems 6.1 and 6.2 to look at what happens when the dimensions of a 1-2-3 box are multiplied by various scale factors. If each dimension is multiplied by the same number, the resulting box is similar to a 1-2-3 box.

Launch

Ask the class what they think will happen to the volume and surface area of a 1-2-3 box if its dimensions are tripled or quadrupled.

> If you tripled each dimension of a 1-2-3 box, what would happen to the surface area? *(It would increase by 9 times, or 3^2.)* How do you know?

> If you tripled each dimension of a 1-2-3 box, what would happen to the volume? *(It would increase by 27 times, or 3^3.)* How do you know?

> How much plywood would be needed to make the new box? How many pounds of garbage could the new box decompose?

Let the class offer a few conjectures. If no one has an idea, just tell them that these types of questions are what they will be exploring in this problem.

Review the information in the student edition about similar figures and scale factors. Have students explore the problem and follow-up in groups of three or four.

Explore

You might ask each member of each group to design one box that is similar to a 1-2-3 box. The students in each group should work together to find the volumes and surface areas of all the boxes that the group designs.

Summarize

If students are struggling with this problem, you may need to further discuss the properties of similar rectangles. The idea of similar rectangular prisms should follow naturally.

Have students describe their similar boxes. It might be informative and helpful to collect their data in a chart.

Scale factor	Length (feet)	Width (feet)	Height (feet)	Volume (cubic feet)	Surface area (square feet)
1	1	2	3	6	16
2	2	4	6	48	64
3	3	6	9	162	144
4	4	8	12	384	256

Help the class to summarize what they have found.

What happens to the volume of a box if its dimensions are tripled? *(The volume will be 27 times as great. It would take 27 of the original boxes to fill the new box.)* What happens to the volume if the dimensions are quadrupled? *(The volume will be 64 times as great. It would take 64 of the original boxes to fill the new box.)*

What happens to the surface area of a box if its dimensions are tripled? *(The surface area will be 9 times as great.)* What happens to the surface area if the dimensions are quadrupled? *(The surface area will be 16 times as great.)*

Ask questions to assess how well students are grasping the ideas of similarity and scale factor as applied to three-dimensional figures.

What are the dimensions, surface area, and volume of a box similar to a 1-2-3 box if the scale factor is 9? *(The dimensions are 9 feet by 18 feet by 27 feet. The surface area is $16 \times 9^2 = 1296$ square feet, and the volume is $6 \times 9^3 = 4374$ cubic feet.)*

What are the dimensions of a box that is similar to a 1-2-3 box but has a surface area of 1600 square feet? What is the scale factor from the 1-2-3 box to the new box? *(The surface area of a 1-2-3 box is 16 square feet, so the scale factor from the small box to the large box is 10. This means that new box's dimensions are 10 feet by 20 feet by 30 feet.)*

What are the dimensions of a box that is similar to a 1-2-3 box but has a volume of 10,368 cubic feet? What is the scale factor from the 1-2-3 box to the new box? *(The scale factor is 10,368 ÷ 6 = 1728. We need to find a number whose cube is 1728. We know that 10^3 is 1000, so it must be greater than 10 but not much. 11^3 is 1331, and 12^3 is 1728, so the scale factor is 12. The new box's dimensions are 12 feet by 24 feet by 36 feet.)*

If the scale factor from a 1-2-3 box to a larger box is 4, how many 1-2-3 boxes will fit in the large box? *(The new box will hold 4 × 4 × 4 = 64 of the 1-2-3 boxes.)*

ACE questions 19–21 involve similar cylinders and could be discussed in class. ACE question 22 also makes a good class discussion. It involves the comparison of the measurements of a model ship to those of the actual ship and makes use of similar plane figures as well as rectangular prisms and cylinders.

Additional Answers

Answers to Problem 6.1

A.

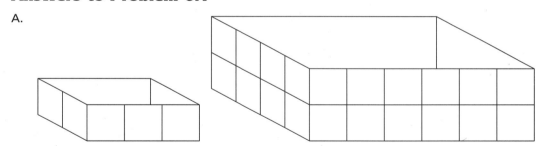

Answers to Problem 6.1 Follow-Up

1. All of these ratios are $\frac{1}{2}$.

2. The surface area of the 1-2-3 box is 16 ft²; the surface area of the 2-4-6 box is 64 ft². The ratio is $\frac{16}{64}$ or $\frac{1}{4}$.

3. The volume of the 1-2-3 box is 6 ft³; the volume of the 2-4-6 box is 48 ft³. The ratio is $\frac{6}{48}$ or $\frac{1}{8}$.

Answers to Problem 6.2 Follow-Up

1. Possible answer: A 1-3-4 box would require 26 ft^2 of plywood.

2. They will need twice the amount called for in the 1-2-3 box recipe: 20 pounds of paper and 30 quarts of water.

3. They will need twice the number of worms: 2000 worms (2 pounds).

Answers to Problem 6.3

C. 1. Possible answer: 1.5-3-4.5 box, 20.25 ft^3; 3-6-9 box, 162 ft^3; 4-8-12 box, 384 ft^3; As a 1-2-3 box has a volume of 6 ft^3, these boxes have, respectively, 3.375 times, 27 times, and 64 times as much volume.

2. The volume grows by the cube of the scale factor.

Finding Volumes of Irregular Objects

In Problem 7.1, Displacing Water, students explore how to find the volume of an irregularly shaped object by measuring the amount of liquid it displaces when placed in a container of water. This technique is used in science and should provide a connection for students. In the process of experimenting, students look at the relationship between milliliters and cubic centimeters.

Mathematical and Problem-Solving Goals

- **To estimate the volume of an irregularly shaped object by measuring the amount of water it displaces**

- **To understand the relationship between a cubic centimeter and a milliliter**

Materials		
Problem	For students	For the teacher
All	Graphing calculators	Transparency 7.1 (optional)
7.1	Clear plastic containers marked in milliliters (such as graduated cylinders; 1 per group), metric rulers (if the containers do not have metric scales), centimeter cubes (5–10 per group), stones and other irregularly shaped objects, clay spheres from Investigation 5 (optional), water	Transparent 2-quart measuring container and a stick of butter (optional)

Student Pages 68–72   Teaching the Investigation 72a

Displacing Water

At a Glance

**Grouping:
small groups**

Launch

■ Tell the story of Archimedes.

Explore

■ Have groups find the amount of water displaced by a centimeter cube and then experiment with irregularly shaped objects.

Summarize

■ Help students summarize the water-displacement method for measuring volume and the relationship between cubic centimeters and milliliters.

■ Talk about the relationship between the increase in the water level and the volume of water displaced.

■ Have students find the volumes of their spheres from Investigation 5. *(optional)*

■ Show how cooks measure shortening. *(optional)*

Finding Volumes of Irregular Objects

You have solved many problems in which you had to calculate the volume or surface area of a prism, a cylinder, a cone, or a sphere. However, many three-dimensional objects do not have such regular shapes. In this investigation, you will explore finding volumes of odd-shaped, or irregular, objects.

7.1 ### Displacing Water

According to legend, Archimedes, a Greek scientist in the third century B.C., made an important discovery while taking a bath. He noticed that the water level rose when he sat down in the tub. He figured out that he could calculate the volume of his body—or any other object—by submerging it in water and finding the difference between the combined volume of the water and the object, and the volume of the water alone. This difference in volumes is called *water displacement.* It is said that Archimedes was so excited about his discovery that he jumped from his bath and, without dressing, ran into the streets shouting "Eureka!"

Think about this!

Does Archimedes' discovery suggest a way to measure the volume of an irregular shape?

In this problem, you measure the volume of water in *milliliters,* a unit commonly used to express the volume of liquids. As part of the problem, you will figure out how to convert milliliters to cubic centimeters.

Assignment Choices

ACE questions 1–7 and unassigned choices from earlier problems

Problem 7.1

You will need a measuring box or cylinder with milliliter markings, water, a few centimeter cubes, and some odd-shaped objects like stones.

Fill the measuring container about halfway with water. Record the volume of the water in milliliters.

To find the volume of an object, drop it into the container and find the volume of water that is displaced. That is, find the difference between the combined volume of the water and the object, and the volume of the water alone.

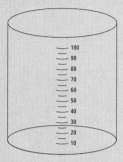

A. How much water is displaced when you drop a centimeter cube into the container? What does this tell you about the relationship between one milliliter and one cubic centimeter?

B. Use this method to find the volume in cubic centimeters of some odd-shaped objects.

■ **Problem 7.1 Follow-Up**

Give examples of objects whose volume cannot be measured by this method. Explain why this method would not work.

Answers to Problem 7.1

A. A centimeter cube displaces 1 ml of water, so 1 ml equals 1 cm³.

B. Answers will vary.

Answer to Problem 7.1 Follow-Up

For the method to work, the object must be completely submerged. Objects that are too large or impossible to submerge (say, the World Trade Center) and objects that float (such as a sponge) can't easily be measured this way.

Answers

Applications

1. The increase in volume is $(2.5)^2\pi = 19.6$ cm³, so each marble has a volume of $19.6 \div 5 \approx 3.9$ cm³ or 3.9 ml.

2a. 6 ft³

2b. 6 in

2c. The volume of the stones is one fourth the volume of the box, or $\frac{1}{4} \times 6 = 1.5$ ft³.

3. 100 ft²

4. Possible answer: 5 cm by 5 cm by 10 cm

5a. $9675 \times 0.05 = 483.75$ cm³ or 483.75 ml

5b. $\frac{483.75\ g}{78,000\ g} \times 100 \approx 0.62\%$

As you work on these ACE questions, use your calculator whenever you need it.

Applications

1. A cylinder with a diameter of 5 cm contains some water. Five identical marbles are dropped into the cylinder, and the water level rises by 1 cm. What is the volume of one marble?

2. A rectangular 1-2-3 box is half full of water.

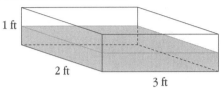

    a. What is the total volume of the box?

    b. What is the water level in the box?

    c. Several large stones are dropped into the box, and the water level rises to $\frac{3}{4}$ full. What is the total volume of the stones?

3. A gallon of paint covers about 400 ft² of surface area. When an artist painted a statue he had carved, he used about 0.25 gallon of paint. What is the approximate surface area of the statue?

4. A rectangular juice box contains 250 milliliters of juice. Give the dimensions of a box that will hold this amount of juice.

5. An average adult has a mass of about 78 kilograms and a surface area of about 9675 cm². A film of water about 0.05 cm thick clings to our skin when we step out of the bath.

    a. What volume of water clings to an average adult when he steps out of the bath?

    b. If 1 cm³ of water has a mass of 1 gram, what percent of an average adult's body mass is the mass of the water that clings to him after a shower?

Extensions

6. Paper often comes in packages of 500 sheets, called reams. A particular ream of paper has a length of 28 cm, a width of 21.5 cm, and a height of 5.5 cm.

    a. What is the volume of a sheet of paper?

    b. What is the thickness of a sheet of paper?

7. A particular iceberg is shaped like a mountain with a height of 1250 m above the water level and a distance of 132 km around the base (1 km = 1000 m) at water level.

    a. What shape most closely resembles the top of a mountain?

    b. Estimate the volume of the part of the iceberg that is above water level.

Extensions

6a. $(28 \times 21.5 \times 5.5) \div 500 \approx 6.6 \text{ cm}^3$

6b. $5.5 \div 500 = 0.011 \text{ cm}$

7a. a cone

7b. The diameter of the base is $132 \div \pi \approx 42 \text{ km}$, so the radius is about 21 km. The volume is approximately $\frac{1}{3} \times \pi \times 21^2 \times 1.25 = 577 \text{ km}^3$.

Possible Answers

1. To find the volume of an odd-shaped object by measuring the amount of water it displaces, you submerge the object and measure how much the water rises. From this measurement and the shape of the container, you can calculate the volume of the water that was displaced. This is also the volume of the submerged object.

2. One cubic centimeter is the same as one milliliter. You can prove this by adding an object that you know has a volume of a certain number of cubic centimeters into a container of water, and measuring how much the volume of the water changes in milliliters. It will be the same number.

Mathematical Reflections

In this investigation, you found volumes of odd-shaped objects by measuring water displacement. These questions will help you summarize what you have learned:

1 Describe how you can find the volume of an odd-shaped object by measuring water displacement, and give an example of a situation in which this method would be useful.

2 What is the relationship between cubic centimeters and milliliters? How can you prove this relationship?

Think about your answers to these questions, discuss your ideas with other students and your teacher, and then write a summary of your findings in your journal.

TEACHING THE INVESTIGATION

7.1 • Displacing Water

In this problem, students will estimate the volume of an irregularly shaped object by measuring the amount of water it displaces.

Launch

Tell the story of Archimedes' discovery. Let students work in groups of two or three on the problem and follow-up.

Explore

Give the class a few minutes to explore water displacement on their own. Some students have been known to drop all their objects—stones and unit cubes—in at once to see the water rise. After the class has had a little time to investigate informally, have them work on the problem to find the volume of an object by the water-displacement method.

Students are first asked to find the amount of water displaced by a centimeter cube. Depending on the container, they may have to drop more than one cube in the water to see a change in the water level. If five cubes are submerged, the water will rise by 5 milliliters. Therefore, 1 cubic centimeter cube is equivalent to 1 milliliter. Once students have this understanding, they can find the volumes of irregularly shaped objects.

Summarize

Ask questions to help the class summarize what they have learned through their experimentation.

> What is the relationship between milliliters and cubic centimeters?

> What objects cannot by measured by the water-displacement method? *(objects that are too large, too inaccessible, or that float)*

Discuss the relationship between the water displaced—as measured by its height—and the increase in the volume. For example, if students are using a cylindrical container, the volume of water displaced is the height the water rises multiplied by the area of the base of the cylinder.

You may want to have the class determine the volumes of some of their spheres of modeling dough from Investigation 5 by using the water-displacement method.

Some cooks use the concept of water displacement to measure shortening, dropping the shortening into a container of water until they have the desired rise in height. You may want to demonstrate this technique using butter or margarine and a transparent 2-quart measuring container.

The Unit Project

Package Design Contest

The Worldwide Sporting Company wants new package designs for its table-tennis balls (Ping-Pong balls). The company's table-tennis balls are about 3.8 cm in diameter. There are three main requirements for the packages:

- The board of directors wants to have three different size packages: small, medium, and large.
- The president of the company wants the cost of the packages to be a primary consideration.
- The sales manager wants the packages to be appealing to customers, to stack easily, and to look good on store shelves.

The company holds a package design contest, and you decide to enter.

- You must design three different packages for the table-tennis balls.
- You must submit your designs and a written proposal to WSC.
- You must try, in your written proposal, to convince WSC to use your designs.

Include the following things in your proposal:

1. A description of the shape or shapes of the packages and an explanation for why you selected these shapes.

2. Patterns for each package that, when they are cut out, folded, and taped together, will make models of your packages. Use centimeter grid paper to make your patterns.

3. Cost estimates to construct your designs. The packaging material costs $0.005 per square centimeter.

4. An explanation of how you have addressed WSC's requirements.

Remember, you are trying to convince WSC that your designs are the best and that they meet the requirements. Your written proposal should be neat, well organized, and easy to read so that the company officials can follow your work and ideas easily.

Assigning the Unit Project

The optional unit project gives students an opportunity to apply what they have learned about volume and surface area in a real-world application problem. In the project, the fictitious Worldwide Sporting Company is sponsoring a contest for the design of three packages to hold standard table-tennis balls. To enter the Package Design Contest, students are to submit three package designs and a written explanation of the designs to the company.

The blackline master for the project appears on page 87. A suggested scoring rubric and samples of student work are given in the Assessment Resources section:

Assessment
Resources

For Check-Up 1, each student will need a sheet of inch grid paper for question 6.

For the quiz, have $8\frac{1}{2}$-by-11-inch sheets of paper and tape available for students who want to use them for question 1.

For the optional Unit Project, students will need centimeter grid paper and, if possible, a few table-tennis balls.

Check-Up 1

This flat pattern can be folded on the dashed lines to make a box.

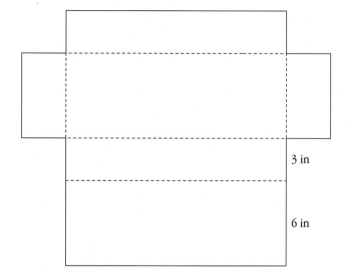

3 in

6 in

15 in

1. What will the surface area of the box be?

2. What will the volume of the box be?

Sweet-Tooth Chocolates is marketing a special assortment of caramels. They want to put 16 individual caramels in the box. Each caramel is 1 cubic inch.

3. List all the ways that 16 caramels can be neatly packaged in a box.

4. Which arrangement of caramels would require the most cardboard for the box?

5. Which arrangement of caramels would require the least cardboard for the box?

6. On grid paper, draw a flat pattern for the box you described in question 5.

Check-Up 2

A rectangular prism and a cylinder are shown below.

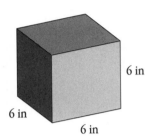

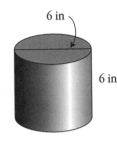

6 in

6 in

6 in

6 in

6 in

6 in

1. Which of the shapes has the greater volume? How much greater? Show how you found your answer.

2. Which of the shapes has the greater surface area? How much greater? Show how you found your answer.

3. If you stacked layers of unit cubes and parts of unit cubes inside each shape, how many layers would you need to fill each shape?

4. Could you put more unit cubes on one layer covering the base of the rectangular prism or the base of the cylinder? How many more? Show how you found your answer.

Check-Up 2

The Athletic Club sells popcorn at school athletic events. They have been using cylinder-shaped containers with a 2-inch radius and an 8-inch height. Their supplier has suggested that they could also sell popcorn in cone-shaped containers with the same dimensions.

5. How much popcorn will the cylinder-shaped container hold if it is filled to the rim?

6. How much popcorn will the cone-shaped container hold if it is filled to the rim?

7. What is the difference between the amount the cylinder will hold and the amount the cone will hold?

8. The Athletic Club wants to adopt the new container and they want to give customers the same value for their money. They used to charge $1.00 for the cylinder-shaped container filled with popcorn. To charge customers a price proportional to the original price, what should they charge for the cone-shaped container?

Quiz

1. Jackie has an $8\frac{1}{2}$-by-11-inch sheet of paper. She wants to use the paper, without cutting it, to make a container with the greatest possible volume. (She will make the top and bottom from another sheet of paper.) She thought of rolling the paper to make an open-ended cylinder and realized that there are two ways to do this. Her friend Renate suggests folding the paper to make a rectangular prism with square ends. Jackie points out that there are also two ways to fold the paper to make the sides of a prism with a square base.

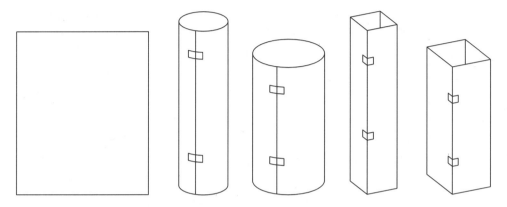

a. Which of the four containers has the greatest volume? You may want to make models of the containers to help answer this question.

b. What is that container's volume?

c. How much greater is this container's volume than the volume of the other container of the same height?

d. Write a note to Jackie explaining why this container has the greatest volume.

Quiz

In 2–10, use this information: Kola Kola is planning to package their cola in a new party-size can in addition to their regular can.

The regular can has a radius of 3 cm and a height of 12.5 cm. The party-size can has a radius of 18 cm and a height of 37.5 cm.

2. How many square centimeters of aluminum are needed to make the regular can? (Assume Kola Kola's cans have flat bottoms and tops.)

3. How many square centimeters of aluminum are needed to make the party-size can?

4. How many cubic centimeters of cola will the regular can hold?

5. How many cubic centimeters of cola will the party-size can hold?

Quiz

6. How many times greater is the radius of the party-size can than the radius of the regular can?

7. How many times taller is the party-size can than the regular can?

8. How many times more square centimeters of aluminum are needed to make just the side (not the bases) of the party-size can than to make the side of the regular can? Explain why the party-size can requires this many *times* more aluminum. (Be specific. Don't just say "because it is bigger.")

9. How many times more cubic centimeters of cola will the party-size can hold than the regular can will hold? Explain why the party-size can holds this many *times* more cola. (Be specific.)

10. If a regular can sells for 35¢, what should the price of the party-size can be if the company wants to base the price on the amount of cola the can will hold?

Assign these questions as additional homework, or use them as review, quiz, or test questions.

1. Sterling Sports manufactures high-quality basketballs. They package their basketballs in 1-cubic-foot cardboard boxes. The basketballs fit nicely in the boxes, just touching the sides. To keep the ball from being damaged, Sterling fills the empty space in the box with foam. How much foam is put in each basketball box?

2. The Spitzleys are going to put a rectangular pool in their backyard. The cost of excavating the dirt (digging up the dirt and taking it away) is $4200. If the hole that is dug has dimensions of 25 m by 15 m by 3 m, what is the cost for the excavation per cubic meter?

3. Make a sketch of a rectangular box with a base of 3 ft by 5 ft and a height of 7 ft.
    a. How many unit cubes would fit in a single layer at the bottom of the box?
    b. How many identical layers of unit cubes could be stacked in the box?
    c. What is the volume of the box?

4. Cement is sold by the cubic yard. A cubic yard of cement is the amount of cement that would fit into a box 1 yd long, 1 yd wide, and 1 yd high. How many cubic yards of cement are needed to make a rectangular patio 9 yd long, $6\frac{1}{2}$ yd wide, and 6 in ($\frac{1}{6}$ yd) thick?

5. Mali keeps her favorite amethyst in a cubic box with a volume of 343 cm^3. What is the surface area of her box? Show enough work so that someone can follow along and know what numbers you used and where the numbers came from.

6. The Tennis for Champs company is looking into new ways to package tennis balls. The packaging engineer at the company is exploring options for vacuum packing the balls (removing the air from the containers in which they are packaged) so they will retain a good bounce. She wonders how much air there is in a standard container of tennis balls. Find the amount of empty space in a cylindrical container that is 18 cm tall and contains three tennis balls 6 cm in diameter.

In 7–11, use this information: Ms. Wohlshied has to purchase paper cups and containers of water for the track-and-field competition. She knows that students often use a cup only once and then throw it away. She buys cone-shaped cups because they are nice for holding, don't hold very much water (which she thinks is good, as students often don't finish the water in their cups), and don't cost very much. This is an illustration of the cups she buys.

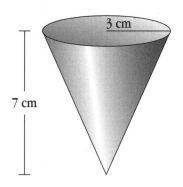

7. How many cubic centimeters of water does the cone-shaped cup hold?

8. If Ms. Wohlshied buys water in 1-liter jugs, about how many cups can be filled from one jug of water? (1 liter = 1000 cubic centimeters)

9. How many times greater is the volume of a cone with a radius of 6 cm and a height of 7 cm than the volume of Ms. Wohlshied's cup?

10. How many times greater is the volume of a cone with a radius of 3 cm and a height of 14 cm than the volume of Ms. Wohlshied's cup?

11. How many times greater is the volume of a cone with a radius of 6 cm and a height of 14 cm than the volume of Ms. Wohlshied's cup?

Unit Test

The Apple Theater concession sells two sizes of popcorn, a micro box and a jumbo box. Answer questions 1–5, and remember to show enough work so that someone reading your paper will know how you found your answers.

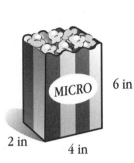

6 in
MICRO
2 in
4 in

JUMBO
12 in
4 in
8 in

1. About how many square inches of cardboard are needed to make the micro box?

2. About how many square inches of cardboard are needed to make the jumbo box?

3. How many cubic inches of popcorn will fit in the micro box if the top of the popcorn is level with the top of the box?

4. How many cubic inches of popcorn will fit in the jumbo box if the top of the popcorn is level with the top of the box?

5. If the micro box sells for 75¢, what should the price of the jumbo box be if it is based on the amount of popcorn the box holds?

Unit Test

6. One face of a cube has an area of 25 cm².

   a. What is the surface area of the cube?

   b. What is the volume of the cube?

7. These are scale drawings of two cylinders. One cylinder has a base circumference of 36 cm and a height of 22 cm. The other cylinder has a base circumference of 22 cm and a height of 36 cm.

   a. Do the cylinders have the same volume? Show your calculations.

   b. Do the cylinders have the same surface area? Show your calculations.

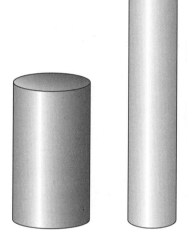

8. This is a sketch of the nose cone of the delivery system for a new satellite. Find its volume.

8 ft

8 ft

diameter of base = 10 ft

Optional Unit Project: The Package Design Contest

The Worldwide Sporting Company wants a new set of package designs for their table-tennis balls (Ping-Pong balls). The company's table-tennis balls are about 3.8 cm in diameter. WWS has decided to offer a scholarship to the students or groups of students who convince the company to use their design.

WWS has three main concerns:

- The board of directors wants a small package, a medium package, and a large package of table-tennis balls.

- The president of the company is concerned about the cost of the packages and wants it to be a primary consideration in the package design.

- The marketing division wants the packages to be appealing to customers, to stack easily, and to look good on store shelves.

You are to prepare an entry for the package design contest. Your task is to design three different packages for table-tennis balls. You will submit your designs and a written proposal to WWS. Your written proposal should try to convince WWS that your designs are the ones they should use.

Include the following things in your contest entry:

1. A description of the shape or shapes of the packages you have designed and an explanation for why you selected these shapes.

2. Patterns for each of your packages that, when they are cut out, folded, and taped together, will make models of your packages. Use centimeter grid paper to make your patterns.

3. Calculations of how much each of your package designs will cost to construct. The packaging material costs $0.005 per square centimeter.

4. An explanation of how you have addressed WWS's three concerns (listed above).

Remember, you are trying to convince WWS that your designs are the best and that they should select your work. Your report is to be written to the company officials. You need to think about the presentation of your written proposal. It should be neat (maybe even typed!), well-organized, and easy to read so that the company officials can follow your work and ideas easily.

Notebook Checklist

Journal Organization

_____ Problems and Mathematical Reflections are labeled and dated.

_____ Work is neat and is easy to find and follow.

Vocabulary

_____ All words are listed.   _____ All words are defined or described.

Check-Ups and Quiz

_____ Check-Up 1

_____ Check-Up 2

_____ Quiz

Homework Assignments

_____   _____

_____   _____

_____   _____

_____   _____

_____   _____

_____   _____

_____   _____

_____   _____

_____   _____

_____   _____

_____   _____

_____   _____

_____   _____

_____   _____

Self-Assessment

Vocabulary

Of the vocabulary words I defined or described in my journal, the word _____ best demonstrates my ability to give a clear definition or description.

Of the vocabulary words I defined or described in my journal, the word _____ best demonstrates my ability to use an example to help explain or describe an idea.

Mathematical Ideas

In *Filling and Wrapping,* we looked closely at two measures for three-dimensional shapes: how much material is needed to *fill* a shape and how much material is needed to *wrap* a shape.

1. a. After studying the mathematics in *Filling and Wrapping,* I learned the following things about volumes and surface areas of prisms, cylinders, cones, and spheres:

    b. Here are page numbers of journal entries that give evidence of what I have learned, along with descriptions of what each entry shows:

2. a. These are the mathematical ideas I am still struggling with:

    b. This is why I think these ideas are difficult for me:

    c. Here are page numbers of journal entries that give evidence of what I am struggling with, along with descriptions of what each entry shows:

Class Participation

I contributed to the class discussion and understanding of *Filling and Wrapping* when I . . . (Give examples.)

Answer Keys

Answers to Check-Up 1

1. 306 in²

2. 270 in³

3. 1 by 4 by 4, 1 by 2 by 8, 1 by 1 by 16, and 2 by 2 by 4

4. the 1 by 1 by 16 box (66 in²)

5. the 2 by 2 by 4 box (40 in²)

6. Possible flat pattern:

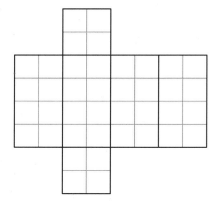

Answers to Check-Up 2

1. *rectangular prism:* $6 \times 6 \times 6 = 216$ in³, *cylinder:* $\pi \times 3^2 \times 6 \approx 169.6$ in³; The rectangular prism has the greater volume (by about 46.4 in³).

2. *rectangular prism:* $6 \times 36 = 216$ in², *cylinder:* $(2 \times \pi \times 3^2) + (6 \times \pi \times 6) \approx 169.6$ in²; The rectangular prism has the greater surface area (by about 46.4 in²).

3. Each shape would hold six layers of cubes.

4. The area of the rectangular prism's base is 36 in², so 36 cubes would cover it. The area of the cylinder's base is $\pi \times 3^2 \approx 28.3$ in², so about 28.3 cubes would cover it. You could put about 7.7 more cubes on the base of the rectangular prism.

5. $\pi \times 2^2 \times 8 \approx 100.5$ in³

6. $\frac{1}{3} \times 100.5 \approx 33.5$ in³

7. about 67 in³ more

8. The cone holds one third as much as the cylinder, so the price should be one third the price of the cylinder, or about 33¢.

Answers to the Quiz

1. **a.** the short cylinder

    b. radius = $11 \div 2\pi \approx 1.75$ in, so volume = $\pi \times 1.75^2 \times 8.5 \approx 81.8$ in^3

    c. The short prism has a volume of $2.75^2 \times 8.5 \approx 64.3$ in^3, so the short cylinder has about 17.5 in^3 more volume.

    d. Answers will vary.

2. about 292 cm^2 of aluminum

3. about 6277 cm^2 of aluminum

4. about 353 cm^3 of cola

5. about 38,170 cm^3 of cola

6. 6 times greater

7. 3 times taller

8. The side of the party-size can requires 18 times more aluminum than the side of the regular can. The circumference (the length of the lateral surface) of the party-size can is 6 times greater than that of the regular can, because the scale factor from the small can's radius to the large can's radius is 6. The height (the width of the lateral surface) increases by a scale factor of 3. Thus, the surface area increases by a scale factor of $6 \times 3 = 18$. This can also be found by dividing the areas: $\frac{4241}{235.6} \approx 18$.

9. The party-size can will hold 108 times more cola than the regular can. The scale factor from the small can's radius to the large can's radius is 6, and the area of the base increases by the square of that scale factor, or 36. The height increases by a scale factor of 3. Thus, the volume increases by a scale factor of $36 \times 3 = 108$. This can also be found by dividing the volumes: $\frac{38,170}{353} \approx 108$.

10. The price should increase by the same scale factor as the volume, or 108, so the price should be $\$0.35 \times 108 = \$37.80$.

Answers to the Question Bank

1. The box's volume is 1 ft^3. The basketball's volume is $\frac{4}{3}\pi \times (\frac{1}{2})^3 \approx 0.52$ ft^3. Each box contains approximately $1 - 0.52 = 0.48$ ft^3 of foam.

2. The volume of the dirt removed is $25 \times 15 \times 3 = 1125$ m^3, at a cost of $\frac{4200}{1125} \approx \$3.73$ per cubic meter.

3. **a.** 15 cubes

    b. 7 layers

    c. 105 ft^3

4. $9 \times 6\frac{1}{2} \times \frac{1}{6} = 9.75$ yd^3 of cement

5. The volume of the box is 343 cm^3, so each edge has a length of 7 cm ($7 \times 7 \times 7 = 343$). One face of the box has an area of $7 \times 7 = 49$ cm^2, so the total surface area is $6 \times 49 = 294$ cm^2.

6. *volume of the container:* $\pi \times 3^2 \times 18 \approx 509$ cm^3, *volume of one tennis ball:* $\frac{4}{3} \times \pi \times 3^3 \approx 113$ cm^3, *volume of air:* approximately $509 - (3 \times 113) = 170$ cm^3

7. $\frac{1}{3} \times 7 \times 3^2 \times \pi \approx 66$ cm^3

8. $1000 \div 66 =$ about 15 cups (Students might suggest 16 or 17, reasoning that the cups would not be completely filled.)

9. As $\frac{1}{3} \times \pi \times 6^2 \times 7 \approx 264$ cm^3, the volume is 4 times greater.

10. As $\frac{1}{3} \times \pi \times 3^2 \times 14 \approx 132$ cm^3, the volume is 2 times greater.

11. As $\frac{1}{3} \times \pi \times 6^2 \times 14 \approx 528$ cm^3, the volume is 8 times greater.

Answers to the Unit Test

1. about 80 in^2

2. about 320 in^2

3. about 48 in^3

4. about 384 in^3

5. From the micro box to the jumbo box, the volume increases by a scale factor of 8, so the price of the jumbo box should be $8 \times 0.75 = \$6.00$.

6. a. 150 cm^2

   b. 125 cm^3

7. a. The radius of the wide cylinder is $\frac{36}{2\pi} \approx 5.7$ cm, so the area of the base is $\pi(5.7)^2 \approx 102$ cm^2, and the volume is approximately $102 \times 22 = 2244$ cm^3. The radius of the narrow cylinder is $\frac{22}{2\pi} \approx 3.5$ cm, so the area of the base is $\pi(3.5)^2 \approx 38.5$ cm^2, and the volume is $38.5 \times 36 \approx 1386$ cm^3. The volumes are not the same.

   b. The wide cylinder has a surface area of $2(\pi \times 5.7^2) + (36 \times 22) \approx 996$ cm^2. The narrow cylinder has a surface area $= 2(\pi \times 3.5^2) + (22 \times 36) \approx 869$ cm^2. The surface areas are not the same.

8. The volume of the cylinder section is $\pi \times 5^2 \times 8 \approx 628$ ft^3. The volume of the cone section is $\frac{1}{3} \times 628 \approx 209$ ft^3. The total volume of the nose cone is approximately $628 + 209 = 837$ ft^3.

The final assessment for *Filling and Wrapping* is a unit test. Below is a suggested scoring rubric and a grading scale for the unit test. They are followed by samples of student work and a teacher's comments on each sample.

Suggested Scoring Rubric

This rubric employs a scale with a total of 18 possible points. You may use the rubric as presented here or modify it to fit your district's requirements for evaluating and reporting students' work and understanding.

As you review the rubric and the student work, note that students are not penalized twice for an error. If a student derives a value that is needed to find another solution, and that value is incorrect, and then carries out a correct procedure with the incorrect value, he or she is given credit for the correct procedure.

- **5 points (questions 1–5)**
  1 point for each correct answer (Half credit is given for partially correct solutions, such as if a student found the surface area for a closed box instead of an open box. Also, half credit is given for a correct response with no work.)

- **2 points (question 6)**
  1 point for each correct answer to parts a and b

- **5 points (question 7, part a)**
  2 points for finding the volume of each cylinder and 1 point for correctly comparing them (Finding this volume is more complex because students are given the circumference of the cylinder and must first find the radius. The point for comparing the volumes is awarded based on the calculations students found.)

- **3 points (question 7, part b)**
  1 point for finding the surface area of each cylinder and 1 point for correctly comparing them (The point for comparing the surface areas is awarded based on the calculations students found.)

- **3 points (question 8)**
  1 point for finding the volume of the cylinder section, 1 point for finding the volume of the cone section, and 1 point for finding the total volume

Grading Scale

Points	Grade
16 to 18	A
14 to 15	B
12 to 13	C
9 to 11	D

Sample 1

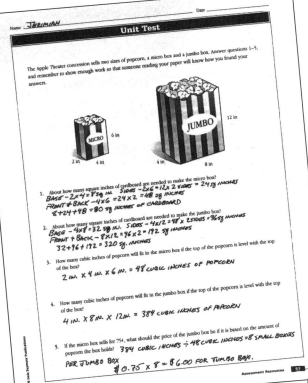

Sample 2

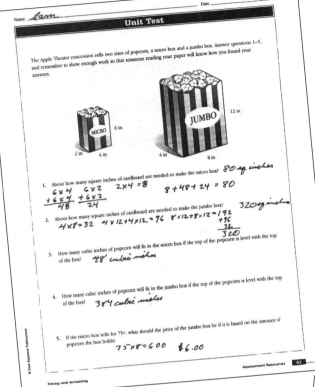

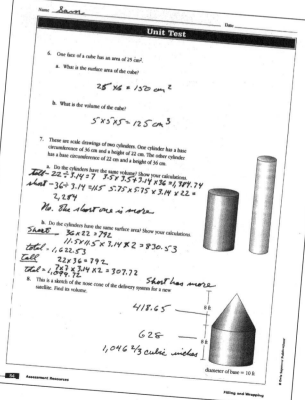

Guide to the Unit Test

Teacher's Comments on Jeremiah's Unit Test

Jeremiah received 16 of the 18 points for the test. Jeremiah shows how he calculates his answers for all of the questions. This made it easy for me, as a teacher, to follow what he did and to see where he made errors.

Jeremiah correctly answers questions 1–6 and question 8.

For question 7 part a, Jeremiah makes a small error when finding the volume of the narrow cylinder. He multiplies the area of the base by π to get the volume instead of multiplying by the height of 36. I believe that Jeremiah knows how to and can find the volumes of cylinders correctly because he does so for the wide cylinder. I took away 1 point for this error because his answer is incorrect and he should have reasoned that something was wrong—the volumes he calculates for the two containers are so very different. We talk a lot in my class about reasonableness of errors, and I expect my students to employ that kind of thinking whenever they work on problems. For question 7 part b, Jeremiah has found the surface area of only the lateral surface of the two cylinders, forgetting the bases even though the problem states that these are closed cylinders. Because I know he can find the area of these bases (he has to for part a of this problem), I have taken off only 1 point for this error instead of taking off 1 point for each incorrect surface area. Also, I gave him credit for the comparison he makes between the two surfaces areas because, based on his solutions, he has given a correct response.

The work Jeremiah has done on this test indicates to me that he has made sense of the ideas presented in this unit.

Teacher's Comments on Sam's Unit Test

Sam received $14\frac{1}{2}$ of the 18 points for this test. Sam is inconsistent in showing how he found his solutions, for which he loses $1\frac{1}{2}$ points (1 point for questions 1–5 and half a point for question 8).

Sam correctly answers questions 1–6 and question 7 part a.

For question 7 part b, Sam makes a small error when finding the surface area of each cylinder, using the diameter of the base instead of the radius. I don't know why he does this; he correctly found the areas of the two bases to answer part a. Because he makes the same mistake in both and because of what he has done in part a, I did not take away 1 point for each of his answers for part b. Instead, I took off a total of 1 point for incorrect surface areas.

For question 8, Sam correctly finds the volume of the cylinder section (though he does not show his work or how he got this answer) but does not find the correct volume for the cone section. Because the volume of the cone is incorrect, the total volume is incorrect. I have taken off only 1 point because the total volume he gives is correct for the volumes he has found.

The work Sam has done on this test indicates to me that he has made sense of the ideas presented in this unit but needs to show his work and be more careful with his calculations.

Guide to the Optional Unit Project

The optional Unit Project gives students an opportunity to apply what they have learned about volume and surface area in a real-world application problem. In the project, the fictitious Worldwide Sporting Company is sponsoring a contest for the design of three packages to hold standard table-tennis balls. To enter the Package Design Contest, students are to submit three package designs and a written explanation of the designs to the company.

The blackline master for the project appears on page 85. Below are suggested scoring rubrics and specific guidelines for how they can be applied to assessing the project. A teacher's comments on two students' work follow the suggested rubrics.

Suggested Scoring Rubrics

The rubrics that follow are written as if Worldwide Sporting Company were evaluating the students' projects. The evaluation consists of two reviews. The first review is essentially a checklist that lets students know whether their proposal has met the company's requirements. The second review is a more thorough evaluation of their mathematics and presentation of ideas, with greater weight placed on the demonstration of mathematical ideas. The teacher who developed these rubrics had her students work in teams but write individual reports. Thus, each student's work was evaluated using these rubrics.

If this were a real review conducted by a real company, entrants who did not meet the requirements of the first review would probably be dropped from the contest. In this learning experience, however, students who do not pass the first review are asked to revise their work until it does pass. All work will eventually be evaluated using both rubrics.

The teacher who developed these rubrics gave students two grades, one for each review. The first grade was based on the score each student received for the first review. (A student's original work was used to determine this grade regardless of whether the student had to revise the work.) The second grade was based on the score each student received for the final review. (Since students could not reach this level until they had passed the first review, only work that had passed the first review was graded using this rubric.)

Sample Packages

The following sample packages will help you to review the packages your students design. Table-tennis balls are $1\frac{1}{2}$ inches, or approximately 3.8 cm, in diameter. The sample packages below assume a diameter of 4 cm. In the table, d = diameter and h = height.

Sample Two-ball Packages

Shape	Dimensions (cm)	Surface area (cm²)	Cost	Cost per ball	Package
Cylinder	$d = 4$ $h = 8$	125.7	62.8¢	31.4¢	
Rectangular prism	4 by 4 by 8	160	80¢	40¢	

Sample Four-ball Packages

Shape	Dimensions (cm)	Surface area (cm²)	Cost	Cost per ball	Package
Cylinder	$d = 4$ $h = 16$	226.2	$1.13	28.3¢	
Rectangular prism	4 by 8 by 8	256	$1.28	32¢	
Rectangular prism	4 by 4 by 16	288	$1.44	36¢	

Sample Eight-ball Packages

Shape	Dimensions (cm)	Surface area (cm²)	Cost	Cost per ball	Package
Cylinder	$d = 4$ $b = 32$	427.3	$2.14	26.7¢	
Rectangular prism	8 by 8 by 8	384	$1.92	24¢	

Grading Scales

The teacher used the following grading scales for the two parts of the project.

First Review

Points	Grade
8 to 9	A
7	B
6	C
4 to 5	D

Note: Students who did not receive an A on the first review had to revise their work before it entered the final review.

Final Review

Points	Grade
24 to 27	A
20 to 23	B
16 to 19	C
12 to 15	D

First Review of Your Package Designs

Thank you, _____, for submitting a set of package designs for our table-tennis balls. Below is a summary of your project's review by our evaluators. This first review evaluates whether you met the requirements for the contest.

Does the proposal includes the following?

Packages in three sizes (small, medium, and large)	**yes**	**no**
Description of the shapes of the packages	**yes**	**no**
Explanation of why these shapes were selected	**yes**	**no**
Cost per package	**yes**	**no**
Description of the cost-efficiency of the designs	**yes**	**no**
Description of appeal and stackability of the designs	**yes**	**no**

Are patterns that could produce the described containers included?

Small pattern	**yes**	**no**
Medium pattern	**yes**	**no**
Large pattern	**yes**	**no**

Each circled **yes** earns 1 point. You must have earned 8 or 9 points to move on to the next level of review. Your score is _____ points.

_____ Congratulations! Your project has made it through the first review. You are now in the finals for the scholarship judging.

_____ Our evaluators feel that your project does not meet the requirements set by our company. Please revise and resubmit your design.

Sincerely,

Worldwide Sporting Company

Final Review of the Package Designs

In the final review, entries are judged in three categories: shape selection, measurement, and presentation.

Rubric for Shape Selection and Measurement

This rubric assigns a score from 0 to 3 for each item in the shape selection and measurement categories.

3 **Complete Response** *(meets the demands of the project)*
- Shows understanding of the mathematical concepts and procedures
- Satisfies all essential conditions of the project

2 **Partial Response** *(work needs some revision)*
- Shows some understanding of the mathematical concepts and procedures
- Satisfies most of the essential conditions of the project

1 **Inadequate Response** *(student needs some instruction to revise work)*
- Shows little understanding of the mathematical concepts and procedures
- Fails to address essential conditions of the project

0 **No attempt**
- Irrelevant response
- Does not address the conditions of the project

Rubric for Presentation

This rubric assigns a score from 1 to 3 for each item in the presentation category.

3 **Complete Response** *(meets the demands of the project)*
- Complete, with clear, coherent work and written explanation

2 **Partial Response** *(work needs some revision)*
- Reasonably complete; may lack detail or clarity in work or written explanation

1 **Inadequate Response** *(student needs some instruction to revise work)*
- Incomplete; work or written explanation is insufficient or not understandable

Shape Selection

The shape (or shapes) selected for the packages are judged on three criteria:

0   1   2   3   Stackability

0   1   2   3   Appeal

0   1   2   3   Cost-effectiveness

Measurements

The measurements given in the report for the proposed packages are judged on four criteria:

0   1   2   3   Measurements are correct for the patterns

0   1   2   3   Measurements are reasonable (table-tennis balls will fit—packages could be slightly larger than actual table-tennis balls, but they cannot be smaller)

0   1   2   3   Amount of material (surface area) is correct for the patterns (numbers may be reasonably rounded)

0   1   2   3   Material cost per package is correct

Presentation (including written proposal and other submitted work)

1   2   3   Neat, easy to read

1   2   3   Organized, easy to follow and to find information

Sample 1

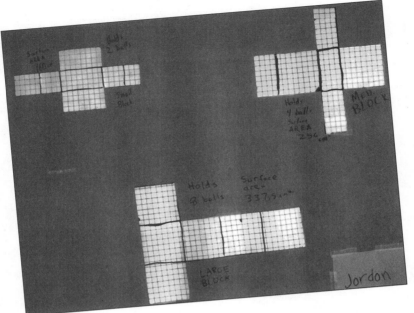

Dear World Wide Sporting Company,

    I saw your contest for making ping-pong ball containers. I started working on a small, medium, and large container.
    The first thing I did was to measure how tall a ping-pong ball was. I discovered it was 4 cm tall. Since it is a sphere and spheres are perfectly round, I knew it was also 4 cm wide. Then I took out 1 cm graph paper. I made a box that was 4 * 4 * 4 cm. I checked to see if a ping-pong ball would fit in it and it did.
    Then I started to make the packages. I made the small package hold two balls. I made it a 4 * 8 * 4 cm box. It was in the shape of a rectangle so it would be easy to stack. There were 5 sections of 4 * 8 cm on the flat pattern. So to find the surface area I did (4 * 8) * 5. That equaled 160 sq cm for the surface area. To find the price I multiplied 160 * 0.005. That equaled $0.80 for the packaging cost.
    I chose the medium package to hold 4 balls. It was a 8 * 8 * 4 cm box. It's an easily stackable rectangle. To figure out the surface area I looked and saw there were four 4 * 8 cm sides. It also had two 8 * 8 cm sides. So my equation was (4 * 8 * 4) + (8 * 8 * 2). That equaled 256 sq cm for the surface area. So to figure out the cost I took 256 * 0.005. That equaled $1.28 for packaging costs.
    I had the large container fit 8 balls. It was the most cost efficient because it was a cube. It was also cheaper because I had each ball take up 3.75 cubic cm. It is a 7.5 * 7.5 * 7.5 cm. The flat pattern had six 7.5 * 7.5 cm sides. So I multiplied 7.5 * 7.5 * 6. That equaled 337.5 sq cm for the surface area. Then I took 337.5 * 0.005. That equaled $1.69 and 3/4 of a cent for packaging costs.
    So these are the ping pong boxes I chose. They are easily stackable and cost efficient.

Sincerely,

Jordon

Jordon

Balls Held	Dimensions	Packaging Cost	Cost Per Ball
2	4*8*4	$0.80	$0.40
4	8*8*4	$1.28	$0.32
8	7.5*7.5*7.5	$1.6875	$0.2109375

Sample 2

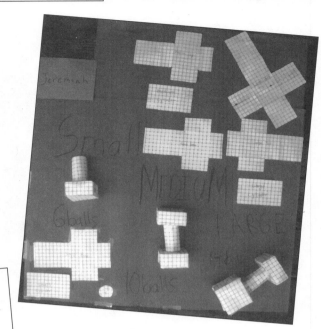

Dear President of WWS,

Our group has designed a set of 3 ping pong ball packages.

Our small package holds 6 ping pong balls, our medium holds 10 ping pong balls, and our large holds 14 ping pong balls. Each of our containers are designed in a dumbell shape. The reason behind this shape is that it doesn't waste a lot of space , is stackable, and defineately will catch the eyes of consumers. Rectangular boxes waste no space, but are not as appealing and besides we want ours to stand out. A consumer may be looking to buy ping pong balls or just be browsing. When the walk by they will stop and say "what is that" as they see these packages. This will increase business and you will soar over the competition. On our included posters are the cut outs and the finished boxes. Each container has more than one pattern that go together to form the finished box. Here are the statistics:

The small package has a 12x7 cutout for the cylinder and a cap, together this will cost $.48. It also has a 7x7x3.5 base that holds 4 ping pong balls, this costs $.98. The small package costs a total of <u>$1.46.</u>

The medium container has a 7x7x3.5 base holding 4 ping pong balls at $.98. It has an identical top which also costs $.98. In between the two idential pieces is a cylinder holding 2 balls which cost $.42. The medium container cost a total of <u>$2.38.</u>

The large container has a 7x7x7 cube for a base that holds 8 ping pong balls and costs $1.47. It has a 7x7x3.5 top that holds 4 ping pong balls and costs $.42. The large container costs a total of <u>$2.87.</u>

We feel that these containers are fairly efficient on space and don't cost a lot in manuracture. We also think that you will think they are more eye catching than the competitions packages. They can probably stack in many different ways. When we thought about stacking we found all of them can be stacked in a pyramid. The area you have to put them in will depend on how many you use on the first level. We would suggest a 3x3 with a 2x2 on top of that and 1 on the top. In boxes the small containers can have one layer right side up, and a layer on top of that upside down. The medium and large can just be stacked layer on layer. I hope you consider our plans for an efficient, stackable, and eye catching line of packages. We think they are quite appealing, hope you think so and are sure the public would think so. Here is a table of information about size cost and dimensions.

Size	# of balls	base/$	top/$	cylinder $	total $
Small	6	7x7x3.5 $.98	none	(+cap) $.48	$1.46
Medium	10	7x7x3.5 $.98	7x7x3.5 $.98	3.5x7 $.42	$2.38
Large	14	7x7x7 $1.47	7x7x3.5 $.98	3.5x5 $.42	$2.87

Sincerely,

Jeremiah

Teacher's Comments on Jordon's Project

First Review

Jordon's report somewhat addresses each of the concerns presented by WWS, though it does not directly explain why the shape he selects for his containers is a reasonable shape (in terms of its shape) or how the shape of his container has appeal. I made small comments on these two issues to let him know what his report was lacking. I thought about having him revise his work but decided not to. This project was assigned to my students during the second semester. As a class, we have spent a lot of time talking about the quality of their work. I have given my students several opportunities to revise and have tried to push them to raise their standards. I decided to let Jordon's work go to the final review stage as is and have him deal with the comments and scores he receives in the final review.

Final Review

Jordon earned 19 of the 27 points for the final review, for a C+. Jordon was surprised by this but, after reading the comments, he seemed to understand the grading. Jordon is a bright student but sometimes settles for less-than-thorough work.

His score was reduced because he never mentions the appeal of his package design from either a customer's or a manufacturing point of view. He makes no attempt in his report to convince WWS to select his package designs. Also, his report is not well-organized. It is difficult for the reader to make sense of some of the numbers he presents. For example, he states there are 5 sections of 4 by 8 rectangles in his flat pattern for his small box. Actually, there are 3 sections that are 4 by 8, 1 section that is 4 by 7, and 1 section that is 4 by 9. The last two sections of the pattern make up one side and part of the top of the box. None of this is explained in his report. Another mathematical problem in his report is that he first uses 4 cm for the diameter of the balls and then, for the larger packages, he uses 3.75 cm. He does not explain why he has changed the number he is using for the diameter of the ball.

Teacher's Comments on Jeremiah's Project

First Review

Jeremiah's report addresses each of the concerns presented by WWS except for the cost-efficiency of the design. Jeremiah also created actual models of his designs, not just patterns. Although that is not rewarded in this first review, this does affect the number of points he receives in the final review.

Final Review

Jeremiah earned 22 of the 27 points for the final review, for a B. Jeremiah lost points for the stackability of his packages but gained points for appeal, not just because of the unusual shape but because of his explanation for why his packages are appealing. The cost of each package is reasonable based on the numbers he uses (3.5 cm for the diameter of a table-tennis ball). However, the packages are really too small to hold actual table-tennis balls; Jeremiah loses points from the measurement section because of this. The added complexity of putting these packages together and the extra material needed to fasten the sections together is not mentioned, but I feel that these ideas are beyond the consideration of most seventh graders.

Blackline Masters

Flat Patterns

Box P

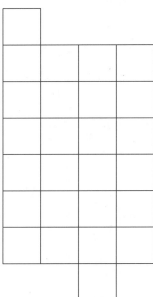

Box Q

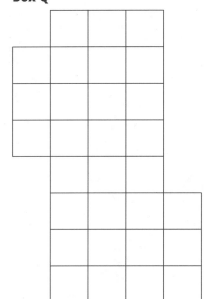

Box R

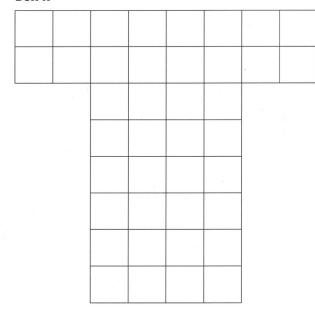

ACE Questions 6 and 7

i.

unit square

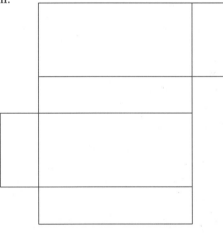

ii.

iii.

Flat Pattern for a Cylinder

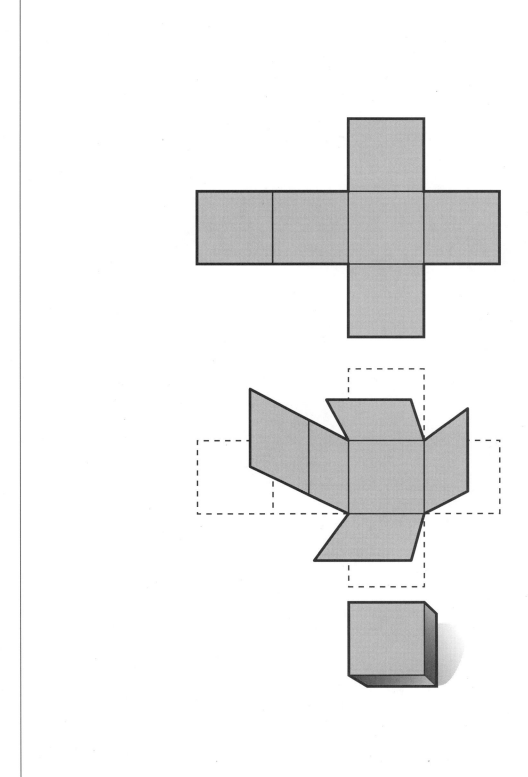

A. How many different flat patterns can you make that will fold into a box shaped like a unit cube? Make a sketch of each pattern you find on inch grid paper. Test each pattern by cutting it out and folding it into a box.

B. Find the total area of each pattern.

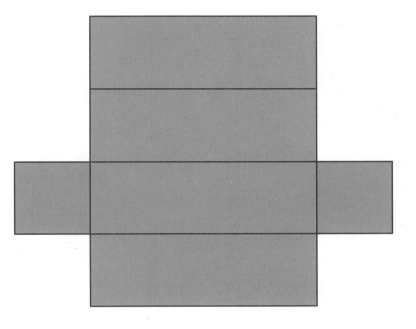

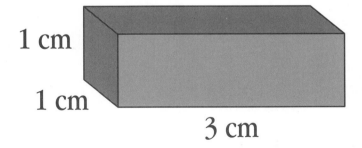

1 cm

1 cm

3 cm

A. On grid paper, draw two different flat patterns that make the same rectangular box. Each side length of your pattern should be a whole number of units. Test each pattern by cutting it out and folding it into a box.

B. Find the total area of each flat pattern you made in part A.

C. Describe the faces of the box formed from each flat pattern you made. What are the dimensions of each face?

D. How many unit cubes will fit into the box formed from each flat pattern you made? Explain how you got your answer.

A. Find the dimensions of your box in centimeters.

B. Use the dimensions you found in part A to make a flat pattern for your box on grid paper.

C. Cut your box along the edges so that, when you lay it out flat, it will match your flat pattern from part B.

Box P

Box Q

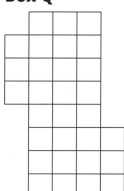

Box R

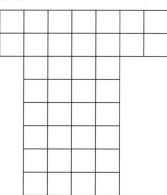

A. Cut out each pattern on Labsheet 1.4, and fold it to form a box.

B. Find the dimensions of each box.

C. How are the dimensions of each box related to the dimensions of its faces?

D. Find the total area of all the faces of each box.

E. Fill each box with unit cubes. How many unit cubes does it take to fill each box?

A. Find all the ways 24 cubes can be arranged into a rectangular prism. Make a sketch of each arrangement you find, and give its dimensions and surface area. It may help to organize your findings into a table like the one below.

Possible Arrangements of 24 Cubes

Length	Width	Height	Volume	Surface area	Sketch
			24 cubic inches		
			24 cubic inches		
			24 cubic inches		

B. Which of your arrangements requires the box made with the least material? Which requires the box made with the most material?

When packaging a given number of cubes, which rectangular arrangement uses the least amount of packaging material?

To help you answer this question, you can investigate some special cases and look for a pattern in the results. Explore the possible arrangements of the following numbers of cubes. For each number of cubes, try to find the arrangement that would require the least amount of packaging material.

8 cubes   27 cubes   12 cubes

Use your findings to make a conjecture about the rectangular arrangement of cubes that requires the least packaging material.

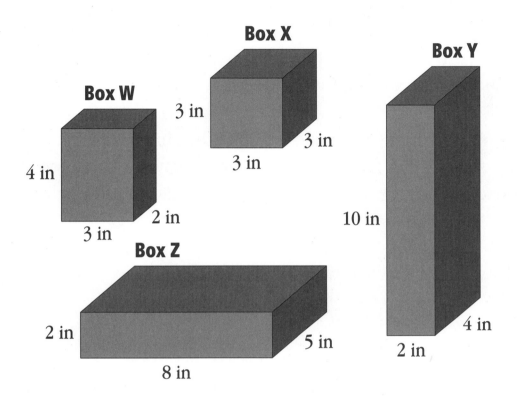

ABC Toy Company is considering using one of Save-a-Tree's ready-made boxes to ship their blocks. Each block is a 1-inch cube. ABC needs to know how many blocks will fit into each box and the surface area of each box.

A. How many blocks will fit in each of Save-a-Tree's ready-made boxes? Explain how you got your answer.

B. What is the surface area of each box? Explain how you got your answer.

The city of Greendale has set aside a piece of land on which to bury its garbage. The city plans to dig a rectangular hole with a base measuring 500 feet by 200 feet and a depth of 75 feet.

The population of Greendale is 100,000. It has been estimated that, on average, a family of four throws away 0.4 cubic foot of compacted garbage a day. How could this information help Greendale evaluate the plan for a waste site?

A. How much garbage will this site hold?

B. How long will it take before the hole is filled?

In Problems 3.1 and 3.2, you saw that you could find the volume of a rectangular prism by figuring out how many cubes would fit in a single layer at the bottom of the prism and then figuring out how many layers it would take to fill the prism. Do you think this layering method would work for finding volumes of different types of prisms?

A. Find the volumes of the triangular, square, pentagonal, and hexagonal prisms you made in cubic centimeters. Describe the method you use.

B. Imagine that each of your paper prisms had a top and a bottom. How would you find the surface area of each prism? Which of the four prisms would have the greatest surface area?

Make a cylinder by taping together the ends of a sheet of paper. Use the same size paper you used to make the prism shapes in Problem 3.3.

A. Set the cylinder on its base on a sheet of centimeter grid paper. Trace the cylinder's base. Look at the centimeter squares inside your tracing. How many cubes would fit in one layer at the bottom of the cylinder? Consider whole cubes and parts of cubes.

B. How many layers of cubes would it take to fill the cylinder?

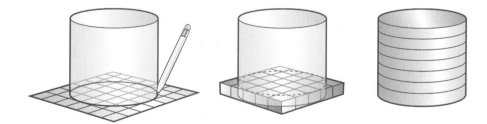

C. What is the volume of the cylinder?

Cut out the flat pattern from Labsheet 4.2. Try to cut the pattern so there is a small connector between each circle and the rectangle.

A. What will the dimensions of the cylinder be?

B. What will the surface area of the cylinder be? Explain how you got your answer.

C. Tape the flat pattern together to form a cylinder. How many centimeter cubes will exactly fit in one layer at the bottom of the cylinder? How many cubes will exactly fill the cylinder?

Fruit Tree decides to try packaging their juice in rectangular boxes.

Fruit Tree wants the new rectangular box to have the same volume as the current cylindrical can.

A. On centimeter grid paper, make a flat pattern for a box that would hold the same amount of juice as the cylindrical can.

B. Cut out your flat pattern. Use colored pencils or markers to design the outside of the box so it will appeal to potential customers. When you are finished, fold and tape your pattern to form a box.

C. Give the dimensions of your box. Are there other possibilities for the dimensions? Explain.

- Using modeling dough, make a sphere with a diameter between 2 inches and 3.5 inches.

- Using a strip of transparent plastic, make a cylinder with an open top and bottom that fits snugly around your sphere. Trim the height of the cylinder to match the height of the sphere. Tape the cylinder together so that it remains rigid.

- Now, flatten the sphere so that it fits snugly in the bottom of the cylinder. Mark the height of the flattened sphere on the cylinder.

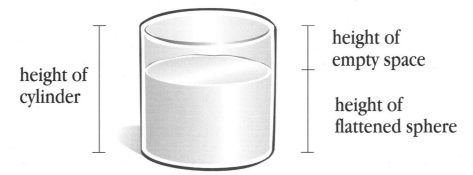

height of cylinder

height of empty space

height of flattened sphere

A. Measure and record the height of the cylinder, the height of the empty space, and the height of the flattened sphere.

B. What is the relationship between the volume of the sphere and the volume of the cylinder?

- Roll a piece of paper into a cone shape so that the tip touches the bottom of your cylinder.

- Tape the cone shape along the seam and trim it to form a cone with the same height as the cylinder.

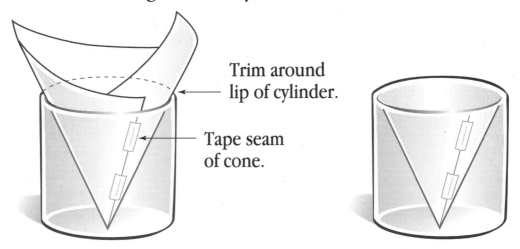

Trim around lip of cylinder.

Tape seam of cone.

- Fill the cone to the top with sand or rice, and empty the contents into the cylinder. Repeat this as many times as needed to completely fill the cylinder.

What is the relationship between the volume of the cone and the volume of the cylinder?

Olga gets a scoop of ice cream in a cone, and Serge gets a scoop in a cylindrical cup. Each container has a height of 8 centimeters and a radius of 4 centimeters, and each scoop of ice cream is a sphere with a radius of 4 centimeters.

A. If Serge allows his ice cream to melt, will it fill his cup exactly? Explain.

B. If Olga allows her ice cream to melt, will it fill her cone exactly? Explain.

Deshondra decides to double each edge of the 1-2-3 box.

A. Use grid paper to make scale models of a 1-2-3 box and Deshondra's 2-4-6 box. The boxes should have open tops.

B. Deshondra wants to increase the composting capacity of her box by the same factor as the volume. How much shredded paper and water will she need for her 2-4-6 compost box?

C. How many worms will she need?

D. How much plywood will she need to build the box?

E. How many pounds of garbage will the box be able to decompose in one day?

How could Ms. Fernandez's class scale up the recipe for the 1-2-3 box to make a box that will decompose 1 pound of organic waste each day?

A. What box dimensions would give the required space for the new quantity of organic waste?

B. Use grid paper to make a scale model of a box that would decompose 1 pound of garbage per day. The box should have an open top.

A. Find three other rectangular boxes that are similar to a 1-2-3 box, and give their dimensions. Give the scale factor from a 1-2-3 box to each box you find.

B. **1.** Calculate the surface area of each box you found in part A, and tell how the result compares to the surface area of a 1-2-3 box.

2. How is the change in surface area from a 1-2-3 box to a similar box related to the scale factor from the 1-2-3 box to the similar box?

C. **1.** Calculate the volume of each box you found in part A, and tell how the result compares to the volume of a 1-2-3 box.

2. How is the change in volume from a 1-2-3 box to a similar box related to the scale factor from the 1-2-3 box to the similar box?

You will need a measuring box or cylinder with milliliter markings, water, a few centimeter cubes, and some odd-shaped objects like stones. Fill the measuring container about halfway with water. Record the volume of the water in milliliters.

To find the volume of an object, drop it into the container and find the volume of water that is displaced. That is, find the difference between the combined volume of the water and the object, and the volume of the water alone.

A. How much water is displaced when you drop a centimeter cube into the container? What does this tell you about the relationship between one milliliter and one cubic centimeter?

B. Use this method to find the volume in cubic centimeters of some odd-shaped objects.

Dear Family,

The next unit in your child's course of study in mathematics class this year is *Filling and Wrapping,* which will teach students about measuring surface area and volume.

In the unit, students will learn about designing packages for shipping products and how to make reasonable comparisons when they shop. They will design packages that meet certain conditions. They will make patterns that fold into prisms and cylinders and will find their volume and surface area. They will learn to think of the volume of such objects as layers of cubes, and with additional practice will connect this idea to finding volume by multiplying the area of the base of the shape by its height. The area of the base tells how many cubes will fit in one layer, and the height tells how many layers are needed.

Students will also do experiments to help them understand the volume of cones and spheres.

Here are some strategies for helping your child work with the ideas in this unit:

- Boxes and packages are all around us. Talk with your child about the size and shape of boxes in your home, and ask why they may be shaped as they are.

- Ask your child about the different ways the class has explored to find the surface area and volume of various shapes.

- Look at your child's mathematics notebook. You may want to review the section where your child is recording definitions for new words that he or she is encountering in the unit.

- Encourage your child's efforts in completing all homework assignments.

If you have any questions or concerns about this unit or your child's progress in the class, please feel free to call. We are interested in your child's success in mathematics.

Sincerely,

Estimada familia,

La próxima unidad del programa de matemáticas de su hijo o hija para este curso se llama *Filling and Wrapping* (Llenar y envolver). En ella se enseña a los alumnos a medir el área superficial y el volumen.

Los alumnos aprender·n a diseñar paquetes de los empleados en el transporte de productos y a hacer comparaciones razonadas al ir de compras. Diseñarán paquetes que satisfagan ciertas condiciones. También harán patrones que, al doblarse, formen prismas y cilindros y hallarán su volumen y su área superficial. Aprenderán a considerar el volumen de ese tipo de objetos como si estuviese formado por capas de cubos y, a través de prácticas adicionales, relacionarán dicha idea con la siguiente manera de hallar el volumen: multiplicar el área de la base de la figura por su altura. El área de la base indica el número de cubos que entrarán en una capa mientras que la altura representa el número de capas necesarias.

Además, los alumnos realizarán experimentos que les ayudarán a comprender el volumen de los conos y de las esferas. He aquí algunas estrategias que ustedes pueden emplear para ayudar a su hijo o hija con las ideas de esta unidad:

- Las cajas y los paquetes son comunes en nuestro entorno. Hablen con su hijo o hija sobre el tamaño y la forma de las cajas que tengan en su casa y pregúntenle por qué tienen esa forma.

- Pregúntenle sobre los diferentes métodos que la clase ha explorado para hallar el área superficial y el volumen de distintas figuras.

- Miren su cuaderno de matemáticas. Es recomendable que repasen la sección en la que anota las definiciones de las nuevas palabras que encuentra en la unidad.

- Anúmenle a esforzarse para que complete toda la tarea.

Si ustedes necesitan más detalles o aclaraciones respecto a la unidad o sobre los progresos de su hijo o hija en esta clase, no duden en llamarnos. Nos interesa que su hijo o hija avance en el estudio de las matemáticas.

Atentamente,

Additional Practice

Investigation 1

Use these problems for additional practice after Investigation 1.

1. Below are four flat patterns that will fold into boxes. Flat pattern iii folds into an open box. The other patterns fold into closed boxes. Answer the following questions for each pattern.

   a. What are the dimensions of the box that can be made from the pattern?

   b. What is the surface area of the box?

   c. What total number of unit cubes would be needed to fill the box?

   i.

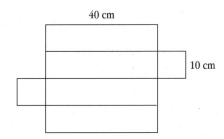

40 cm

10 cm

   ii.

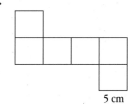

5 cm

   iii.

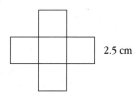

2.5 cm

   iv.

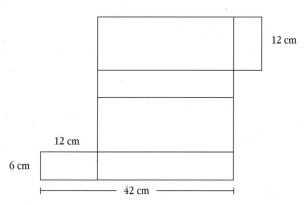

12 cm

12 cm

6 cm

42 cm

2. Gina has a sheet of cardboard that measures 9 ft by 6 ft. She uses scissors and tape to make the entire sheet of cardboard into a closed box that is a perfect cube.

    a. What is the surface area of the box?

    b. What is the length of each edge of the box? Explain your reasoning.

    c. How many unit cubes would it take to fill the box?

3. Bill has a sheet of cardboard with an area of 10 ft^2. He uses scissors and tape to make the entire sheet of cardboard into a closed box. The four sides of the box have the same area, and the two ends have the same area.

    a. The area of each of the four equal sides is twice the area of each end. What is the area of each face of Bill's box?

    b. What are the dimensions of Bill's box?

    c. How many unit grid cubes would it take to fill the box?

Investigation 2

Use these problems for additional practice after Investigation 2.

1. The bottom of a closed box has an area of 50 cm^2. If the box is 8 cm high, give at least three possibilities for the dimensions of the box.

2. The rectangular prism below is made from centimeter cubes.

   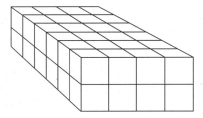

   a. What are the dimensions of the prism?

   b. What is the surface area of the prism?

   c. What is the volume of the prism? That is, how many cubes are in the prism?

   d. Give the dimensions of a different rectangular prism that can be made from the same cubes. What is the surface area of the prism?

3. Use the diagram below to answer the following questions.

   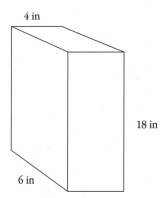

   4 in

   18 in

   6 in

   a. What is the total surface area of the box, including the bottom and the top?

   b. How many inch cubes would it take to fill the box? Explain your reasoning.

4. Each small cube in the rectangular prism below has edges of length 2 cm.

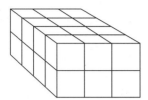

a. What are the dimensions of the prism in centimeters?

b. What is the surface area of the prism in square centimeters?

c. How many 1-centimeter cubes would it take to make a prism with the same dimensions as this prism? Explain your reasoning.

Investigation 3

Use these problems for additional practice after Investigation 3.

1. Answer questions a and b for each closed box below.

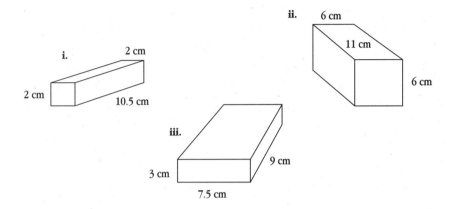

   a. What is the surface area of each box?

   b. What is the volume of each box?

2. What is the volume of the prism below? Explain your reasoning.

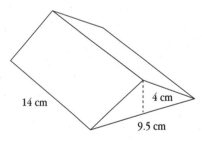

3. The volume of a prism is 275 cm³. The area of the base of the prism is 25 cm². What is the height of the prism? Explain your reasoning.

4. Give the dimensions of three different rectangular prisms that have a volume of 240 cm³.

5. A wading pool is in the shape of rectangular prism with a base area of 15 m² and a depth of 1.25 meters.

   a. What is the volume of the pool?

   b. A hose fills the pool at the rate of 0.75 m³ every 2 minutes. Write a linear equation for the volume of water, *V*, in the pool after *t* minutes.

   c. How much time will it take for the pool to fill? Explain your reasoning.

Investigation 4

Use these problems for additional practice after Investigation 4.

1. The circumference of the base of a cylinder is 16π cm. The height of the cylinder is 10 cm.

   a. What is the surface area of the cylinder?

   b. What is the volume of the cylinder?

2. Use the closed cylinders below to answer each of the following questions.

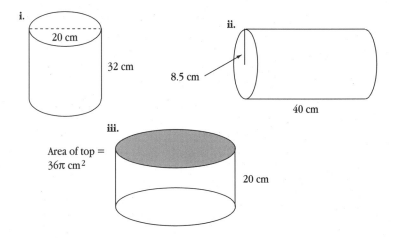

   a. What is the surface area of each cylinder?

   b. What is the volume of each cylinder?

3. A cylindrical storage tank has a radius of 1 m and a height of 3 m. Water flows out of the tank at the rate of 2 m³ every 3 minutes.

   a. What is the surface area of the storage tank?

   b. What is the volume of the storage tank?

   c. The tank starts out full. Write a linear equation for the amount of water, *W*, left in the tank after water has been flowing out for *t* minutes. Explain your reasoning.

   d. What is the slope of your equation in part c? What does the slope represent?

   e. What is the *y*-intercept? What does the *y*-intercept represent?

   f. How much water is left in the tank after 10 minutes?

   g. How long does it take for all the water to flow out of the tank? Explain your reasoning.

4. A cylinder without a top has a height of 25 cm and a circumference of 10π cm.

   a. What is the surface area of the cylinder?

   b. What is the volume of the cylinder?

Investigation 5

Use these problems for additional practice after Investigation 5.

1. Find the volume of each of the following:

    a. a sphere with a radius of 4 cm

    b. a cone with a height of 10 in and a base of radius 3 in

    c. a cylinder with a base area of 10π cm^2 and a height of 25 cm

    d. a sphere with a diameter of 100 cm

    e. a cylinder with a radius of 14 in and a height of 1.5 ft

    f. a cone with a base area of 11.5π cm^2 and a height of 20 cm

2. Find the volume of each of the following figures.

    a.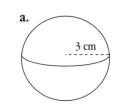

    3 cm

    b.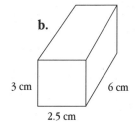

    3 cm   6 cm

    2.5 cm

    c.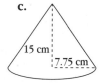

    15 cm   7.75 cm

    d.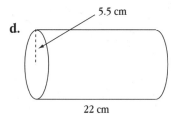

    5.5 cm

    22 cm

3. A tepee is a conical shaped tent used for shelter by the Plains Indians of North America. Suppose a tepee has a radius of 9 ft and is 10 ft high.

    a. How much floor space does the tepee have?

    b. What is the volume of the tepee?

4. Use the diagram below to answer the following questions.

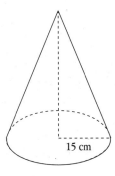 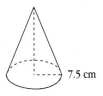

15 cm

7.5 cm

    a. Assuming the two cones are similar, what is the height of the smaller cone?

    b. What is the volume of the larger cone?

    c. What is the volume of the smaller cone?

    d. Angie is using the smaller cone to scoop popcorn into the larger cone. How many scoops from the smaller cone will it take to fill the larger cone?

5. A sphere has a diameter of 4 m. What is its volume?

Investigation 6

Use these problems for additional practice after Investigation 6.

1. A closed rectangular box has a height of 2 ft, a length of 4 ft, and a width of 4 ft.

   a. What is the volume of the box? What is the surface area of the box?

   b. Give the dimensions of a closed rectangular box that has one-fourth the volume of this 2-4-4 box, and give the surface area of this smaller box.

   c. What is the ratio of the surface area of the 2-4-4 box to the surface area of the box you found in part b?

2. Lee built a box with a volume equal to 8 times the volume of a 2-1-5 box.

   a. What might the dimensions of Lee's box be?

   b. Is your answer to part a the only possibility for the dimensions of the larger box? Explain your reasoning.

3. A cone has a height of 12 cm and a base with a radius of 4 cm.

   a. The cone is scaled down to one-eighth of its volume. What are the dimensions of the scaled-down cone?

   b. Is your answer to part a the only possibility for the dimensions of the scaled-down cone? Explain your reasoning.

4. a. How does the volume of a sphere with a radius of 4 cm compare to the volume of a sphere with a radius of 6 cm? Explain your reasoning.

   b. Are the 4-cm sphere and the 6-cm sphere similar? Explain your reasoning.

Investigation 7

Use these problems for additional practice after Investigation 7.

1. Betty dropped 4 cubes into a graduated cylinder partially filled with water. Together the four cubes displaced 21 cm³ of water. If the volumes of the cubes are in the ratio of 3:2:1:1, what is the volume of each cube?

2. When a ball is immersed in water, it displaces 36π cm³ of water. What is the radius of the ball?

3. A conical cup is partially filled with water as shown in the diagram below. Use the diagram to answer the following questions.

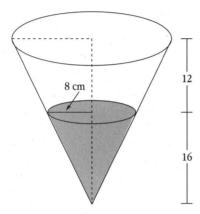

8 cm

12

16

   a. What is the radius of the top of the cup? Explain your reasoning.

   b. What is the volume of the water in the cup?

   c. What is the volume of the cup? Explain your reasoning.

4. When a cube is dropped into a graduated cylinder partially filled with water, the 125 ml of water are displaced. What is the length of each edge of the cube? Explain your reasoning.

Investigation 1

1. **i. a.** 10 cm × 10 cm × 40 cm   **b.** 1800 cm^2 **c.** 4000

    ii. a. 5 cm × 5 cm × 5 cm   **b.** 150 cm^2 **c.** 125

    iii. a. 2.5 cm × 2.5 cm × 2.5 cm   **b.** 31.25 cm^2 **c.** 15.625

    iv. a. 6 cm × 12 cm × 30 cm   **b.** 1224 cm^2 **c.** 2160

2. **a.** 54 ft^2

    b. 3 ft; The sheet of cardboard can be divided into six 3 ft × 3 ft squares. Each square is a face of the resulting box.

    c. 27

3. **a.** Four sides have area 2 ft^2, and two sides have area 1 ft^2.

    b. 1 ft × 1 ft × 2 ft

    c. 2

Investigation 2

1. Possible answer: 8 cm × 5 cm × 10 cm, 8 cm × 2 cm × 25 cm, 8 cm × 4 cm × 12.5 cm

2. **a.** 2 cm × 4 cm × 6 cm   **b.** 88 cm^2 **c.** 48 cm^3

    d. Possible answers: 2 cm × 8 cm × 3 cm; 92 cm^2; 4 cm × 4 cm × 3 cm; 80 cm^2; 1 cm × 8 cm × 6 cm; 124 cm^2

3. **a.** 408 in^2

    b. It would take $6 \times 4 = 24$ cubes to fill the bottom layer and $24 \times 18 = 432$ to fill the box.

4. **a.** 4 cm × 6 cm × 8 cm

    b. 208 cm^2

    c. It would take $6 \times 8 = 48$ cubes to make the bottom layer and $48 \times 4 = 192$ cubes to make the prism.

Investigation 3

1. **i. a.** 92 cm^2 **b.** 42 cm^3

    ii. a. 336 cm^2 **b.** 396 cm^3

    iii. a. 234 cm^2 **b.** 202.5 cm^3

2. The volume is the area of the triangular base times the height, $\frac{1}{2}(4)(9.5)(14) = 266$ cm^3.

3. $V =$ (area of base) $\times h$. In this case, $275 = 25 \times h$, so $h = 11$ cm.

4. Possible answer: 10 cm × 3 cm × 8 cm, 12 cm × 10 cm × 2 cm, and 8 cm × 6 cm × 5 cm

5. **a.** 18.75 m^3

b. $V = \frac{3}{8}t$, or $V = 0.375t$

c. The pool is filled when $0.375t = 18.75$. So $t = \frac{18.75}{0.375} = 50$ minutes.

Investigation 4

1. a. $288\pi \approx 904.8$ cm^2

   b. $640\pi \approx 2010.6$ cm^3

2. i. a. 840π cm^2 b. 3200π cm^3

   ii. a. 824.5π cm^2 b. 2890π cm^3

   iii. a. 312π cm^2 b. 720π cm^3

3. a. 8π m^2

   b. 3π m^3

   c. $W = 3\pi - \frac{2}{3}t$; The tank begins with 3π m^3 and loses $\frac{2}{3}$ m^3 every minute.

   d. The slope is $\frac{-2}{3}$, and it represents the rate of water flow out of the tank in cubic meters per minute.

   e. The intercept is 3π, and it means that, inititally, there are 3π m^3 of water in the tank.

   f. $W = 3\pi - \frac{2}{3} \times 10 = 3\pi - \frac{20}{3} \approx 2.76$ m^3

   g. $0 = 3\pi - \frac{2}{3} \times t$ or $\frac{2}{3} \times t = 3\pi$, so $t = \frac{9\pi}{2} \approx 14.14$ minutes

4. a. $275\pi \approx 863.9$ cm^2

   b. $625\pi \approx 1963.5$ cm^3

Investigation 5

1. a. $\frac{256\pi}{3} \approx 268.1$ cm^3 b. $30\pi \approx 94.2$ in^3

   c. $250\pi \approx 785.4$ cm^3 d. $\frac{4000\pi}{3} \approx 4188.8$ cm^3

   e. $2.04\pi \approx 6.41$ ft^3 f. $76.67\pi \approx 240.9$ cm^3

2. a. $36\pi \approx 113.1$ cm^3 b. 45 cm^3

   c. $300.3\pi \approx 943.5$ cm^3 d. $665.5\pi \approx 2090.7$ cm^3

3. a. $81\pi \approx 254.5$ ft^2 b. $270\pi \approx 848.2$ ft^3

4. a. 14 cm   b. $2100\pi \approx 6597.3$ cm^3

   c. $262.5\pi \approx 824.7$ cm^3 d. 8

5. $\frac{32\pi}{3}$ m^3, or about 33.5 m^3

Investigation 6

1. **a.** $V = 32$ ft^3; $SA = 64$ ft^2

    b. Possible answers: a 2ft × 2ft × 2ft box, which has a surface area of 24 ft^2.

    c. 8:3

2. **a.** Possible answer: $4 \times 2 \times 10$

    b. No, another box would have dimensions $8 \times 2 \times 5$.

3. **a.** height = 6 cm; radius = 2 cm

    b. Yes, the cone in part a is the only possibility because the height and radius must be scaled down by the same scale factor for cones to be similar.

4. **a.** The 6-cm sphere has 3.375 times more volume. The volume increases by the scale factor cubed, $(1.5)^3 = 3.375$.

    b. Yes, the two spheres are similar. All spheres are similar to one another.

Investigation 7

1. The cubes have volume 9 cm^3, 6 cm^3, 3 cm^3, and 3 cm^3, respectively.

2. 3 cm

3. **a.** 14 cm; The ratio of the radius of the water to its height is 8:16. For the height of 12 + 16 = 28 cm, the radius must in the same ratio: 14:28.

    b. $341.3\pi \approx 1072.3$ cm^3

    c. 5747.0 cm^3; The radius at the top is 14 cm, and the height is 28, so volume $= \frac{1}{3}(14^2)(28)\pi = 1829.3\pi \approx 5747.0$ cm^3.

4. The volume of the cube is 125 ml = 125 cm^3. Since $5^3 = 125$, each edge of the cube has a length of 5 cm.

base The bottom face of a three-dimensional shape.

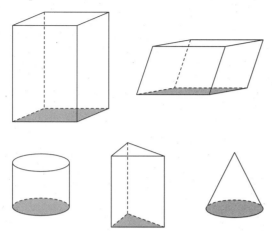

cone A three-dimensional shape with a circular end and a pointed end.

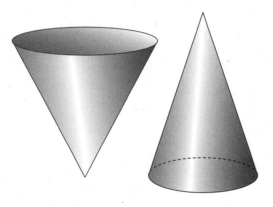

cube A three-dimensional shape with six identical square faces.

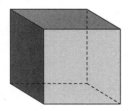

cylinder A three-dimensional shape with two opposite faces that are congruent circles. A rectangle (the lateral surface) is "wrapped around" the circular ends.

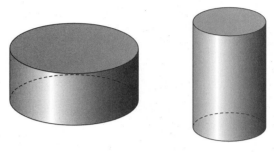

edge The line segment formed where two sides of the polygons that make up the faces of a three-dimensional shape meet.

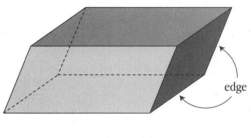

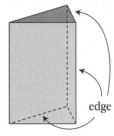

face A polygon that forms one of the flat surfaces of some three-dimensional shapes.

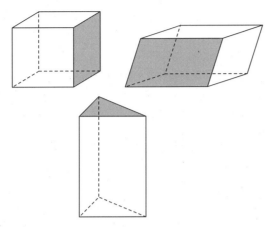

flat pattern An arrangement of attached polygons that can be folded into a three-dimensional shape.

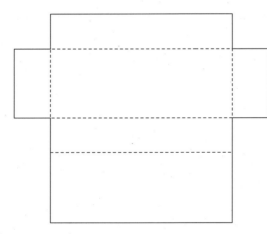

oblique prism A prism whose verticle faces are not all rectangles.

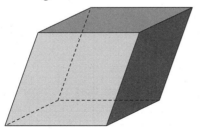

prism A three-dimensional shape with a top and bottom that are congruent polygons and faces that are parallelograms.

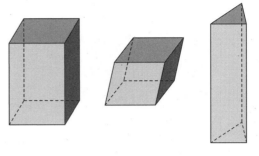

rectangular prism A prism with a top and bottom that are congruent rectangles.

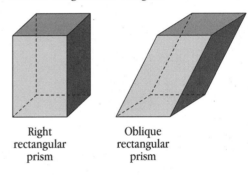

Right rectangular prism

Oblique rectangular prism

right prism A prism whose vertical faces are rectangles.

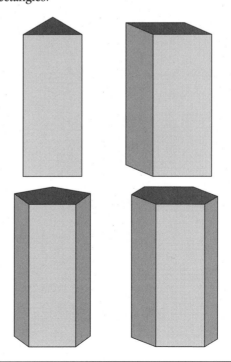

sphere A three-dimensional shape, such as a ball, whose surface consists of all the points that are a given distance from the center of the shape.

surface area The area required to cover a three-dimensional shape. In a prism, it is the sum of the areas of all of the surfaces.

unit cube A cube with all edges equal to one unit in length. It is the basic unit of measurement for volume.

volume The amount of space, or the capacity, of a three-dimensional shape. It is the number of unit cubes that will fit into a three-dimensional shape.

Index